TREVOR BROOKING'S
100
GREAT
BRITISH
FOOTBALLERS

TREVOR BROOKING'S
100
GREAT
BRITISH
FOOTBALLERS

Macdonald
Queen Anne Press

A *Queen Anne Press* BOOK

© Trevor Brooking 1988

First published in Great Britain in 1988 by
Queen Anne Press, a division of
Macdonald & Co (Publishers) Ltd
3rd Floor
Greater London House
Hampstead Road
London NW1 7QX

A member of Maxwell Pergamon Publishing Corporation plc

Jacket photographs – Front: Stanley Matthews *All-Sport*
John Barnes *Colorsport*

British Library Cataloguing in Publication Data

Brooking, Trevor, *1948–*
    Trevor Brooking's 100 great British
    footballers.
    1. Great Britain. Association football –
    Biographies
    I. Title
    796.334′092′2

    ISBN 0–356–14864–5

Typeset, printed and bound by Butler & Tanner Ltd, Frome, Somerset

CONTENTS

BIBLIOGRAPHY

The Glory and the Dream: The History of Celtic FC *Mainstream*
Glory, glory: My life with Spurs by Bill Nicholson *Macmillan*
Rothmans Football League Players' Records 1946–81 *Queen Anne Press*
Soccer Choice by Ron Greenwood and Bryon Butler *Pelham*

PICTURE CREDITS

Aldus Archive: 105
All-Sport: 88, 188, 213; (Simon Bruty) 24; (David Cannon) 30, 77, 190, 198, 214; (Chris
      Cole) 40; (Michael King) 48
Associated Sports Photography: 16, 33, 98, 99, 127, 141, 147, 170, 174, 186, 197, 205
Colorsport: 12, 14, 18, 20, 27, 34, 37, 44, 47, 52, 55, 59, 63, 64, 69, 73, 74, 78, 83, 89, 92,
      94, 102, 104, 108, 110, 111, 116, 117, 119, 121, 123, 128, 130, 132, 137, 143, 145,
      154, 160, 162, 164, 166, 167, 168, 171, 175, 180, 182, 184, 194, 201, 202, 207, 212,
      218, 221
Express Newspapers: 150, 209
Keystone Collection: 56. 86, 90, 114, 139, 152, 220
Press Association: 21
Sporting Pictures (UK) Ltd: 43, 81, 135, 191
Bob Thomas: 51, 60, 67, 70, 95, 126, 155, 158, 178, 216

TREVOR BROOKING BY MICHAEL HART

Few footballers have given me as much pleasure as Trevor Brooking. His was a rare, refined talent, the sort that comes along once every decade and restores your faith in the beautiful game of football. To him, football was an art form and the world his canvas. His loyalty to West Ham perhaps restricted his achievements but, like Bobby Charlton and George Best, he had a distinctive talent that was appreciated by a global audience.

Trevor's 47 caps for England may have earned him international regard, but nowhere was he loved more than in east London. It is an area not noted for the niceties of life, but the supporters of West Ham saw in Brooking a warm and genuine local hero. He was a true sportsman, one of football's gentlemen at a time when the game was becoming increasingly aggressive and physical. In a 17-year career he was cautioned just five times and never sent off. Trevor remains a caring and conscientious ambassador for the game and his reputation and integrity have won him a place as chairman of the Eastern Region of the Sports Council, chairman of the Friends of New Mossford, a Barkingside charity for handicapped children, and as a trustee of the Butler Trust, a prison service awards scheme.

Married with two children, Trevor is also co-director of Colbrook Plastics, leading suppliers of plastic comb binding, and a succinct and shrewd match summariser for BBC radio and television. But it is as a footballer of style and quality that he will be best remembered. In a modern game, relying more and more on power, strength and defensive organisation, he offered a touch of creative class. For me, a lifelong fan, there will never be another Trevor Brooking ... the last of the big splendours.

INTRODUCTION

Some are born great, some achieve greatness and some have greatness thrust upon them.

William Shakespeare

Some footballers are born with a wonderful natural talent, though most have to strive to achieve their greatness. The fame that highlights their stature within the game is invariably thrust upon them. But what is it that makes a 'great' footballer? Is it one who makes 100 League appearances, or scores 100 goals in the First Division or plays 100 times for his country? Most professionals will appear in far more than 100 games, some will score more than 100 goals and a handful will make 100 international appearances. All of them at some stage in their careers, will have been described as a great prospect, played in a great game, scored a great goal or made a great save. Great is probably the most overworked adjective in the football vocabulary. It's inevitable, then, that some people will ask whether there have really been 100 great players in the last 30 years.

By definition, the great player must be outstandingly good at his job, therefore he requires a high level of skill. The truly skilful player lingers in the memory and many of those I've chosen walked straight into the 100 with just a nod of acknowledgment from me. Others had an individual quality, or some outstanding element of their career that demanded inclusion in these pages.

Where did I start? Well, firstly, my 100 players span the era from my schooldays to the present day. They are either footballers I've played with or against or those that I watched and admired as a schoolboy and who had, in their way, some influence on my own development. There were many great footballers before that time and I'm sure that those who saw them play would undoubtedly demand their inclusion. But I felt it was only fair to write about those I had seen personally or played against. Legendary names like Raich Carter, Len Shackleton, Tommy Lawton, Len Goulden, and many more, were players I didn't have the good fortune to see. I've included half a dozen pre-1960s idols whom I watched as a youngster in recognition of what I consider to have been a wonderful era in English football. The heroes of that time inspired many young schoolboys, including me.

It's impossible, in my opinion, to make a definitive comparison between the modern day stars and the likes of Tom Finney and Sir Stanley Matthews. Would players of that era have flourished in the modern game? Undoubtedly, yes. The talent to play football is a timeless quality, all that changes is the fitness level, tactics and techniques. But it is impossible to measure accurately quality and skill. That is why, in the end, it is a matter of personal choice and not everyone will agree that my 100 players all deserve the description great. In making my choice I have considered my own personal recollections, the statistical nuts and bolts of a player's career and, in most cases, I think I have recognised that a great player needs a pretty good supporting cast.

There were three other considerations in making my selection. I have always admired the showmen among footballers, the entertainers who can pull an appreciative crowd to their feet with a moment of magical skill. It helps, too, if they are winners because most great players, from whatever age, shared the will to win. Finally, sentiment played a part in my selection. Loyalty is a fine quality in a footballer and I have always admired the uncomplaining, long-serving professional and there are so many of them in the British game. Had there been no restriction on numbers I would have been happy to include players like John Trollope (Swindon), Jimmy Dickinson (Portsmouth) and Roy Sproson (Port Vale), who all made more than 700 League appearances for just one club. Another stalwart, Alan Oakes, made 777 League appearances for Manchester City, Chester and Port Vale. Others, like my old West Ham team-mate Phil Parkes, Les Chapman, Ron Harris, Ernie Moss and John Wile all played more than 700 League games and are regretted omissions.

There are other personal favourites I've had to leave out, among them many players who were the unsung heroes of their respective teams. West Ham's Ronnie Boyce springs to mind, along with Alan Hinton of Derby, John Fantham (Sheffield Wednesday), Joe Shaw (Sheffield United) and, of course, Paul Madeley of Leeds United and England. I wanted particularly to recognise the contribution that this type of player makes and so included John Jackson, who just edged out Kevin Keelan of Norwich, and George Armstrong, who I plumped for ahead of his Arsenal team-mate Peter Simpson.

Among other reluctant absentees are former West Ham colleague Bryan 'Pop' Robson, a prolific goalscorer who caused me a lot of heart searching. So did Ron Flowers, Keith Weller, Eddie Hopkinson, Mike Bailey, Bobby Collins, George Graham, Sandy Jardine, Tony Brown, Ian Storey-Moore, Freddie Hill, Don Masson, Brian Labone and Tommy Smith. Finally, others like Liam Brady, Johnny Giles, Steve Heighway, Ossie Ardiles and Frans Thijssen had to be left out because my selection was restricted to British players.

For me it was a pleasure and a privilege to play with so many of the great names in the game and to those I have not included in my 100 I would simply say that it is their omission that will generate the biggest debate among readers of this book.

Lastly, I would like to thank Ron Greenwood and Don Howe for sharing their opinions with me on the greats of the 1950s and 1960s. Their reminiscences about the players I admired so much as a youngster were invaluable in plugging the gaps in my memory.

IVOR ALLCHURCH

Ivor Allchurch was one of the all-time great names of Welsh football. I can remember watching him play in the 1960s and the thing that struck me most was his lovely passing ability. One of two famous footballing brothers from Swansea, Ivor was the more gifted player though his younger brother Len was a good enough winger to play for Wales. Ivor was an inside forward, with a neat touch, perceptive dribbling skill and the pace to regularly get him into scoring positions.

Ivor Allchurch MBE (midfield)
Swansea 16.10.29
Swansea City, Newcastle
United, Cardiff City
Wales – 68

Ivor joined Swansea in 1947 but it wasn't until two years after finishing his National Service that he made his League debut. He was an established first team player at Swansea when he played the first of 68 games for Wales at the age of 20. Blessed with a playing style that was simple yet elegant, he became one of the hottest properties in the game in the 1950s and Swansea had to fight to keep him. But, after 11 years and 166 goals in more than 300 games – still the club goal scoring record at Swansea – he moved to Newcastle for £27,000 in 1958.

He was idolised during his four years at St James' Park. Ron Greenwood, my former manager at West Ham and England, recalled, 'You could do nothing but admire him. He was a great prompter, a creative player who could always send his centre forward away with a great through pass. He struck the ball well with either foot which is always a big asset to a player who relies on his passing.'

Whenever I saw him play he always seemed to have time on the ball which is the hallmark of a player with good control. He was stylish, rarely hurried and, when I was a youngster playing an inside forward's role, I used to study Ivor closely to see what it was that gave him so much time on the ball. It was simply that his first touch was always clean and his general level of skill good enough for him to control the ball and select his pass before a defender could challenge him. His long passing was his strength and the fact that he was tall and blond endeared him to the Welsh public and the St James' Park crowd. He scored at the rate of a goal every three games for Newcastle before moving back to Wales and joining Cardiff for £15,000 in August 1962. Three years later he returned to Swansea for a final two seasons before retiring in 1967. For an inside forward he was quite a remarkable marksman. In an 18-year career he scored more than 250 goals which few modern midfield players could emulate.

On the other hand, if he had a weakness, it was the lack of the defensive awareness that has become so much a part of the modern midfield player's game. But when you can score goals at his rate is it important whether you can defend, too?

Anyone who watched Allchurch with Swansea, Newcastle or Wales would have realised that he possessed a rare talent. Unfortunately, his measured, economical style of play is seen less and less in the modern game, where both sets of defences push forward, trying to compress the play into a few yards either side of the halfway line. In these circumstances it's almost impossible for today's players to find the time or space that Ivor enjoyed. Having said that, though, I still believe that he could have adapted to the modern game. His technique, vision and touch would have given him a significant advantage and allowed him to use the ball just as effectively as he did all those years ago.

There are players with natural ability in every era, but Ivor honed his techniques during hours of practice with the ball — something that few youngsters do these days. What has happened, consequently, is that today's young players rely more on their physical attributes than on their skill level, and this is reflected in the game even at the highest levels.

His younger brother played for Swansea, Sheffield United and Stockport and won 11 Welsh caps. Ivor's 68 caps stood as a Welsh record for 20 years until being overtaken by Joey Jones, the Liverpool, Wrexham, Chelsea and Huddersfield full back.

Ivor Allchurch, whose legendary passing ability made a great impression on me in my early days.

JIMMY ARMFIELD

I've chosen Jimmy ahead of some other very fine full backs like George Cohen and Don Howe because of his all-round ability. He was a very cultured right back, sharp in the tackle and quick to recover if his winger went past him. I think I remember him most for his distribution and forays into the opposing half of the field and many observers would argue that he was the originator of the modern technique of overlapping play by full backs. This, of course, is a point that is practically impossible to prove beyond doubt but it is a fact that this is now a long established tactic in the game, whereas before Armfield there were no overlapping full backs.

Jimmy came from Blackpool and spent many of his schooldays playing rugby union. He was destined to be a schoolteacher but his combination of intelligence, speed on the playing field and a natural talent for ball games meant that when Blackpool spotted him playing soccer they immediately invited him to Bloomfield Road for a trial in 1954.

In those days the young Armfield was a right winger, one of a number at Blackpool in the shadow of the immortal Stanley Matthews. Jimmy waited his turn until, one day, a right back was injured in a training game. He deputised in the number two shirt and within a few months was in the first team playing alongside his hero, Matthews. There's little doubt that Jimmy's early days as a winger gave him a taste for the attacking aspects of the game. His natural instinct was to push forward and when he saw the openings, and the time was right, he could use his pace and ability to cross the ball with good effect. Of course, any full back can rush blindly forward; it is the timing of the run that is essential. The full back who plunges forward without thinking leaves his defence vulnerable to a counter-attack. But Matthews, supported by Armfield's diligent overlapping, must have given Blackpool the most feared right wing combination in the First Division. They didn't play together in the same England side though. Matthews' final appearance in a full international came in 1957, two years before the first of Armfield's 43 England caps.

Armfield's debut came just hours after playing for the England Under–23 side in a 3–0 win in Italy. Straight after the match he flew with Jimmy Greaves direct to Rio de Janeiro. Although England lost 2–0 in Brazil, Jimmy made an outstanding job of marking Julinho and immediately established himself as a regular England defender for the next five years, at one stage playing in 37 consecutive matches. Midway through this sequence of games he played for England in the 1962 World Cup in Chile where his composure and constructive use of the ball won him the vote as the finest right back in the world.

One of the most memorable of his games for England was against Spain at Wembley in October 1960 when his armour was tested to the full by one of the world's best palyers of that era – the swift, lightweight Real Madrid winger Francisco Gento. Armfield's domination was total and at

Jimmy Armfield (full back)
Blackpool 21.9.35
Blackpool
England – 43

Jimmy Armfield in action for England against Scotland in 1961. He is widely acknowledged as one of the game's first overlapping full backs.

the end of England's 4–2 win he was given a standing ovation by the Wembley crowd.

He captained England on 15 occasions and, in a 19-year career with Blackpool, played a club record 568 League games. An amiable, humorous, pipe-smoking man, he tried football management with Bolton and Leeds after his retirement. Although a natural leader on the field, I suspect he was too generous a spirit to be totally successful as a football manager.

GEORGE ARMSTRONG

I have always considered little George Armstrong to be one of the unsung heroes of the famous Arsenal side that achieved the League and FA Cup double in 1971. He was a key member of a very fine team and made an enormous creative contribution to the 34 goals shared by twin strikers Ray Kennedy and John Radford that season. He scored seven himself and with Frank McLintock and Bob Wilson was the only player to appear in all 42 League matches.

Armstrong was one of the most industrious players in a very hard working team. He was built like a pit pony and shouldered full responsibility for his share of the workload. His energy was prodigious and he would chase forward to get in crosses and then scurry back to tackle and cover his defenders. He came from Hebburn in the North East and soon after joining Arsenal in 1961 became known as 'Geordie' to his playing colleagues. He wasn't naturally gifted, but he was a player's player — someone who was admired and respected by his fellow professionals. Don Howe, the Arsenal coach in 1971 and later an influential figure in the England coaching set-up, always spoke highly of Armstrong's role at Highbury.

'He was a terrific grafter with enormous stamina', he told me. 'He used to win the cross-country races regularly and it was his running and covering that allowed George Graham to get forward and score so many goals. He was also a wonderful striker of the ball, so good in fact that we used him to take the corners from both sides of the field.'

Although he was more comfortable on the left flank, he could play on either wing and if the opposition had a particularly dangerous wide player George would quite often play on that side to help protect the Arsenal full back. That Arsenal side, managed by Bertie Mee, certainly wasn't among the most entertaining in the game, but Arsenal were very difficult to beat and George was one of the reasons why that was so. He was a small winger who was perpetually buzzing around everywhere. I played against him many times and if you got away from an Arsenal defender it was often George who popped up to save a dangerous situation and you'd think to yourself, 'What the hell is he doing back here?'

I don't think Arsenal realised Armstrong's full value to the side until they tried to replace him when he joined Leicester in 1976. They tried a number of permutations with wingers who couldn't get back to defend or wide midfield players who couldn't get to the line and cross the ball. They spent a lot of money on players like Peter Marinello and spent time on the development of youngsters like Graham Rix. These players all had qualities of their own, of course, but none had the mix that made Armstrong such a complete and invaluable member of the team. He gave Arsenal tremendous service, playing more than 500 games and providing a stream of crosses for players like Radford, Kennedy and Graham to head into the net. It was

George Armstrong (winger)
Hebburn 9.8.44
Arsenal, Leicester City,
Stockport County

his centre from the left flank that Kennedy headed into the Tottenham net for the goal that won the League title in 1971. Five days after that he played on the winning side in the FA Cup final at Wembley. He played at Wembley in the final against Leeds the following year and also played in the Arsenal side that won the old Fairs Cup in 1970.

Although he played for the England Under–23 side, he was never elevated to the senior team which was a shame because I would have enjoyed watching him compete at the very highest level in the game. If I had a criticism of him it was that he didn't score enough goals, though his team-mates in the early 1970s considered that irrelevant. Players like McLintock and Wilson have nothing but praise for George. After 16 years at Highbury, he spent just one season at Leicester before ending his playing days with Stockport County.

George Armstrong, 'a terrific grafter with enormous stamina'. His work-rate played a vital part in Arsenal's 1971 League and FA Cup double.

ALAN BALL

Not only short in stature, Alan Ball was probably the original short-passing midfield player. Sometimes, watching him play, I felt that the shorter the pass the better he liked it. He was phenomenally effective and very influential in a major new trend in the game in the 1960s. The son of an ex-professional, he had begun his career on the wing with Blackpool in the early 1960s but his enormous reserves of energy meant that he was able to cover practically every blade of grass over the 90 minutes.

Ball made his England debut against West Germany in 1965 and his work-rate convinced the manager, Alf Ramsey, that a 4–4–2 formation without orthodox wingers would be the best tactic for the approaching World Cup. So the 'wingless wonders' were born and the success of Ball on the right side of midfield and Martin Peters on the left were key elements in England's triumph in 1966. Ball and Peters established themselves in the side during the build-up to the finals at the expense of wingers like Peter Thompson and Terry Paine and Ramsey perservered with the 4–4–2 formation throughout his career as England manager. Eventually the strategy was copied by practically every club in England.

I think most people remember Alan for his work-rate and the accuracy of his passes, even if they were short ones. His energy level was prodigious and his example was probably responsible for a new breed of hard-running midfield players. It was the sight of him running with his socks down round his ankles during the 1966 World Cup final that endeared him to the public. Ramsey realised that to make his new system work he needed at least two midfield players who could run forward consistently over 90 minutes into attacking positions. Although the system ensured a tighter defensive strategy, the absence of wingers also meant that the team's attacking potential would inevitably suffer. Therefore, the midfield players chosen for this task had to maintain quite prodigious levels of fitness because it was such a physically demanding role. Alan Ball fitted the bill perfectly. He could get forward and link up with the strikers and also had the running power to work back and help the defence when necessary. His all-round ability made the 4-4-2 system effective, and if today's midfield player sometimes curses the workload, Alan is the man he should blame. His commitment and a biting tackle made him a pocket battleship in midfield, a player who would suddenly take command in the heat of the action. Not surprisingly, Everton paid Blackpool £110,000 for him shortly after the World Cup final.

He then became a member of one of the finest midfield trios I have ever seen – Ball, Kendall and Harvey. Together they helped Everton to win the League title in 1970. Alan loved a challenge and, having won a championship medal, decided that he needed a new platform for his talents. In 1971 he moved to Arsenal, who had just won the League and FA Cup double, but he was never to surpass the years he spent at Goodison Park.

Alan Ball (midfield)
Farnworth 12.5.45
Blackpool, Everton, Arsenal,
Southampton, Bristol Rovers,
Portsmouth
England – 72

Ball had a dynamic personality and was a very competitive man, whether he was playing in a World Cup final or a five-a-side match in training. If he had a fault it was his temper. He had a very short fuse and years later, when manager of Portsmouth, his volatile temperament was often apparent, his red hair suddenly emerging from the dug out as he screamed at his players or the referee. His temper got him into a lot of trouble during his playing career but his managers at Blackpool, Everton, Arsenal and Southampton would, I'm sure, all agree that they were always guaranteed a committed performance from Alan Ball.

OPPOSITE *Pocket battleship Alan Ball was a master of the short pass. His running power was a key factor in England's 1966 World Cup victory.*

GORDON BANKS

Gordon Banks OBE
(goalkeeper)
Sheffield 30.12.37
Chesterfield, Leicester City,
Stoke City
England – 73

In terms of goalkeeping quality it is almost impossible to separate Gordon Banks from his protégé, Peter Shilton, but I suspect that Gordon's reputation will survive longer because he was fortunate enough to play in the 1966 World Cup winning team. And, of course, he was good enough to make the save that everyone remembers – in the 1970 World Cup in Mexico, in front of a global television audience. The fact that his most memorable save was against the legendary Brazilian, Pele, guarantees its place in soccer folklore. People still talk about Pele's downward header, Banks' anticipation of the bounce and his full stretch dive to somehow scoop the ball from under the crossbar. It was Banks at his most brilliant, giving a wonderful example of the art of goalkeeping. I remember watching the game on television and seeing England's captain, Bobby Moore, freezing momentarily then clapping in disbelief and finally patting the crouched Banks on the head in a gesture of relief.

Banks was acknowledged as such a crucial part of Sir Alf Ramsey's team in Mexico that when he was ill immediately before the West Germany game there were rumours that his food had been deliberately poisoned in a bid to sabotage England's chances. These were only rumours but his unfortunate absence from that team, and England's subsequent 3–2 defeat against the Germans, meant that his understudy, Peter Bonetti, would spend the rest of his playing career rueing the day he deputised for the great Banks.

Bonetti, the Chelsea goalkeeper and an outstanding performer in his own right, was largely blamed, and never really forgiven, for England's defeat that day. I've always felt that the criticism of Bonetti was unfair though in some ways that incident helped to enhance Banks' reputation. To be honest, though, his reputation didn't really need any boosting. By 1970 Gordon was widely regarded as the best goalkeeper in the world. He was a great shot-stopper and one of these unflappable goalkeepers who always looked in total control no matter how frantic the action in the penalty area.

I think Banks was probably the man who took goalkeeping into the modern age. He began his professional career with Chesterfield in 1958 in the era of cloth caps and baggy shorts, but his concentration and mastery of the techniques of goalkeeping eventually made him one of the great names of world football. He was the man who made goalkeeping glamorous but there was nothing pretentious about him. He was outstanding at his job and accepted the praise with quiet dignity. Even after England's 1966 World Cup final win he remained quite unmoved by the fame.

The Banks legend took root at Wembley in 1966 and his success and amiable personality gave a new aura and stature to goalkeeping. Before Banks goalkeepers seem to have been a bit of an afterthought, but in the 1960s, when Gordon was so influential in England's emergence as a world power in soccer, club managers and coaches began to realise that if they

wanted to build successful teams one of their priorities was to find a top quality goalkeeper. Fortunately, since Banks — and in some ways because of him — England has been blessed with a succession of brilliant goalkeepers. It is the one position our international managers have never had difficulty filling.

Banks had joined Leicester after just one year with Chesterfield and in 1967 he became one of the first big goalkeeping transfers, moving from Filbert Street to Stoke for £52,000. Within a month West Ham had paid a new record fee for a goalkeeper — £65,000 for Bobby Ferguson from Kilmarnock. Gordon's departure from Leicester came about because, amazingly, the club had unearthed another goalkeeper of similar potential. Peter Shilton was then in the youth team and Matt Gillies, the manager at the time, had the unenviable task of deciding whether to stick with Banks or cash in on his reputation and try the precocious young Shilton who was saying 'play me in the first team or I will leave'.

Banks could easily have gone to West Ham because the manager at

The man who brought goalkeeping superstar status. Gordon Banks never over-elaborated and he made his art appear simple.

Upton Park, Ron Greenwood, had an understanding with Gillies that he would have first option should they decide to sell Banks. While Leicester were dithering, Greenwood had also secured an agreement with Kilmarnock for Ferguson. The Scottish club eventually agreed to release Ferguson to West Ham and, although Banks became available shortly afterwards, Ron had already agreed a deal with Kilmarnock and wasn't a man to break his word. So Gordon signed for Stoke and went on to win 73 England caps before a motoring accident effectively ended his career in 1972.

Not long before this accident Gordon had made a memorable penalty save from his World Cup colleague Geoff Hurst in a League Cup semi-final at Upton Park. That was an exhausting series of matches — four in all — but Stoke finally emerged victorious with a 3–2 victory at Old Trafford and went on to beat Chelsea in the final.

JOHN BARNES

John Barnes is the youngest of my 100 players. As a teenager he had the potential to become one of football's great names but, initially, I hesitated over selecting him thinking it a little premature to include him alongside wingers like Matthews, Finney, Best and Coppell. It was his £900,000 transfer from Watford to Liverpool at the age of 23 and the fact that he immediately began producing performances of consistent quality that, finally, demanded his inclusion in these pages on merit alone.

Barnes was born in Jamaica, the son of an army officer who later became military attaché to Great Britain, and John played his early football for Sudbury Court in the Middlesex League. But it wasn't until he came under the critical eye of Graham Taylor at Watford that he began to blossom as a player of outstanding talent. He spent six seasons in the first team at Vicarage Road and, each season, his goal tally reached double figures. In his debut year, 1981–82, he finished as the club's second highest marksman and played a significant role in helping them climb out of Division Two. In 1984 he played in the Watford team that lost 2–0 to Everton in the FA Cup final at Wembley. In those days he looked one of the most skilful young players in the League and it was just a question of whether this rather relaxed and easy going character would have the ambition to make the most of his potential.

Taylor, who can be a dictatorial manager, demanded and, for the most part, got the best out of Barnes. It was no surprise, then, when he was elevated from the Under–21 to the full England squad but it wasn't until a month after that FA Cup defeat by Everton that he really made an impression on the international scene. He couldn't have chosen a more memorable stage – the awesome Maracana Stadium in Rio on a warm, balmy afternoon. England had travelled to South America for three matches in the summer of 1984 after a string of indifferent results against Wales, Scotland and the USSR. I feared a disastrous tour but England beat Brazil, lost to Uruguay and drew with Chile and, for manager Bobby Robson, there was a double bonus – Barnes and Mark Hateley. Both emerged strongly as international class players on that trip and both scored in the 2–0 win in Rio, England's first victory in Brazil.

I was at that match and will never forget the superb goal Barnes scored. It was Brazilian in concept and execution, a searing run carrying him past lunging tackles before he quite casually slid the ball past the goalkeeper. It was typical of this brilliant winger but, sadly, inconsistency, the affliction of so many wingers, cost him a regular place in the England side. He shared the duties with Tottenham's Chris Waddle but, at least, sampled the World Cup atmosphere in the later stages of the quarter final against Argentina in 1986 when he came on as substitute and almost rescued the game for England.

I think that by 1987 Barnes realised that he would only secure further

John Barnes (winger)
Jamaica 7.11.63
Watford, Liverpool
England – 42

significant progress in his career if he moved from Vicarage Road to a bigger club. So when Barnes began agitating for a transfer, his agents took a television video recording of him in action to prospective buyers on the Continent. Barnes favoured a move abroad but in June 1987, when no foreign club had taken the bait, he almost reluctantly signed for Liverpool, who had declared their interest in him from the outset. I feel his flamboyant style would have been appreciated on the Continent but, even so, I was surprised that no other First Division club made a serious attempt to sign him.

But, with Liverpool in 1987–88, he impressively swept away any doubts about his talent or commitment. He helped to make Liverpool the number one attraction wherever they played and, as the first black player to hold down a regular place at Anfield, he quickly endeared himself to the local fans. With typical Liverpool humour they nicknamed him 'Tarmac' – the black Heighway. The move to Liverpool almost immediately established him in the England side and he played a major role in securing England's participation in the 1988 European Championship finals in West Germany.

I would always have him in my England side because he's capable of winning a match with a moment's magic, but I'm not sure that Bobby Robson would share that view. All managers want wingers to work back and although John now has a far greater awareness of his defensive responsibilities I know that in his early days with England he felt that he was called on to defend to the detriment of his attacking game. He is, by nature, an attacking player who is equally at ease on the wing or in a central striking role. Although not a great goalscorer, he is a scorer of great goals – as he showed so spectacularly in Brazil.

He has a wonderful feel for the ball and, when it's knocked in to him, can cushion it almost without thinking. Although predominantly left footed, he can roll and drag the ball both ways and his dribbling routines carry him safely past defenders on either side. His ability to whip in crosses from tight situations with his left foot has considerably enhanced Liverpool's appeal and their goalscoring potential. They have given him what is, in effect, a free role, and, along with the industrious Peter Beardsley, he has transformed them into one of the most entertaining teams in the land. Whether they will be as successful as some of the previous Liverpool sides has yet to be established but, to my mind, they are the most entertaining. Much of the credit for that must go to Barnes, an affable young man who is so enthusiastic about the game that he invested in a television satellite dish for his home simply so that he could watch football from around the world.

But, in 1987–88, the rest of the footballing world was watching him. He was, quite simply, the personality of the season. As Liverpool swept majestically to the League title and FA Cup final, John's enormous contribution was recognised, first by his fellow professionals who named him Player of the Year and then by the Football Writers' Association who voted him Footballer of the Year. It was a remarkable first season at Anfield.

OPPOSITE *John Barnes with the League trophy, won by Liverpool in 1988. As his performance in the European Championship showed, he must be relieved of his defensive duties if he is consistently to recreate his club form at international level.*

JIM BAXTER

Jim Baxter (midfield)
Fife 29.9.39
Raith Rovers, Glasgow
Rangers, Sunderland,
Nottingham Forest
Scotland – 34

Jim Baxter was an exhibitionist and a fine player whose career was flawed by off-the-field controversy. His skill was undeniable, but his love of fame and glamour and a racy reputation contributed, in my opinion, to his downfall. He failed to reach the peaks that his talent deserved. He came from Fifeshire and as a boy earned £6 a week carrying pit props to the coalface. But his potential in junior football was soon spotted and he played briefly for Raith Rovers before joining the mighty Glasgow Rangers for a fee of £12,000.

In five years at Ibrox he became the strutting, arrogant star of Scottish football. Primarily a left half, he was a ball juggler with a flair for taunting opponents, the long decisive pass and the dramatic killer goal. He had a distinctive, loose-limbed stride and used to run on his toes, smoothing his black, Beatle-cut hairstyle. In football mad Glasgow he was the king. He attracted adoring female fans in the way George Best did in Manchester. He was an individual who ran onto the field with his shirt hanging outside his shorts and then proceeded to give a show biz routine of feinting and pirouetting and neat little drag backs. He saw it as almost his duty to entertain.

Baxter's biggest asset was his creative passing from midfield but there were some who didn't appreciate his individualism and called him a stroller. He had a superb touch but I would have to agree that when his team lost possession he didn't go out of his way to help them win back the ball. Like so many very gifted players, he enjoyed a lively private life and had his share of problems off the field. It seems that he also had problems with injuries and with his weight in the later stages of his career with Sunderland and Nottingham Forest.

He played 34 times for Scotland, making his debut against Northern Ireland while with Rangers in 1961. He particularly enjoyed antagonising England defenders. He used to play a game with the late John White called 'Nutmegs'. They would wager on who could slip the ball more often through the legs of England players. Perhaps the most memorable moment in his relatively short career came against England at Wembley in 1963. Playing in a great Scottish side that included Denis Law, Dave Mackay and White, Baxter's left foot wizardry destroyed England. Baxter scored both goals in Scotland's 2–1 win – the second was a penalty. When a team-mate handed him the ball and muttered, 'Mind you score, Jim', he replied coolly, 'Just get back to the centre and line up'.

Two years after that game Baxter finally got his wish and moved from Rangers into the English game. Sunderland, a club of puritanical tradition, paid a record £70,000 and obviously felt they could reform him. They couldn't. He was twice sent off while playing for them and after two years they sold him to Nottingham Forest for £100,000. By this time the Baxter image was fading fast and he was no longer the king of Glasgow. He had

OPPOSITE *Glasgow Rangers'*
strutting midfield artist.
Regrettably, Jim Baxter never
quite fulfilled his potential.

not been the sensation in England that he was in Scotland – he played just 50 games for Forest and, after being suspended for a breach of club discipline, was given a free transfer.

His inability to establish himself at Forest cost him his place in the Scotland squad. He was a victim of his own personality and the changing nature of the midfield player's role. Explaining his decision to release Baxter, the Forest manager of the time, Matt Gillies, said, 'The day of the ball-juggling midfield player has gone. These days he has to win the ball and use it as quickly as possible.' At the age of 30 Baxter rejoined Rangers on a free transfer, four years after leaving them, but he quickly realised that the great days were over and he eventually became a publican not far from Ibrox.

PETER BEARDSLEY

I always remember Kevin Keegan, during his time at Newcastle, talking at length and with great enthusiasm about a young striker called Peter Beardsley. Kevin reckoned that this youngster, whom most people hadn't even heard of, would one day play for England. He was right.

Peter was born in Newcastle and had a rather unorthodox, low key introduction to professional football and that's probably why so few people had heard of him until his return to his home town. He spent the first three seasons of his career with Carlisle before disappearing from the Football League altogether to play for Vancouver Whitecaps in Canada. But he was obviously a youngster with a vast, untapped potential because in 1982 Manchester United took him to Old Trafford. They tried to get the best out of him but failed – he didn't play a single first team game and the following year he returned to Vancouver.

Peter must have been wondering whether he had any future at all in the English game until Newcastle decided to take a chance on him. It was a gamble that paid off handsomely. His goals in 1983–84 – 20 in 35 matches – played a crucial part in helping the club to win promotion from Division Two that season. While at Newcastle he benefited enormously from the guidance and experience of Keegan. They were fortunate at St James' Park to have two youngsters emerging alongside Keegan – one was Peter and the other was Chris Waddle. Although Waddle probably received greater publicity in the promotion year, I recall Kevin telling me that Peter Beardsley was the better all-round player.

I think Peter is now established as a fetcher and provider with few equals in the First Division. He is essentially a front striker, but prefers to play a little deeper. His strength is his willingness and ability to run at defences from deep positions. He is a good dribbler, like his former team-mate Waddle who is now at Spurs. Sadly, it is an art that is in decline, in fact, the word 'dribbling' has almost disappeared from the football vocabulary. Unlike Waddle, who tends to dribble around the outside of defences, Beardsley prefers to attack in the central areas of the field, starting his runs with a little, deceptive swivel of the hips which almost always puts defenders on the wrong foot. It's a great asset, particularly at international level, against man-for-man markers, because having wriggled past one defender his running commits other covering defenders and creates space and opportunities.

If he has a weakness it is that he doesn't score sufficient goals. If he could recapture the scoring rate of the promotion year of 1983–84 he would be the complete striker. Even so, I'm sure that the strikers who play alongside him, like John Aldridge at Liverpool and Gary Lineker with England, would be quick to defend him on this point. Peter has created numerous goals for England in the last two seasons and Gary, who has scored many, is the first to give him credit.

Peter Beardsley (striker)
Newcastle 18.1.61
Carlisle United, Manchester United, Newcastle United, Liverpool
England – 26

Peter made his international debut as a substitute in Egypt in January 1986 but it was in the World Cup in the heat of Mexico five months later that he was to establish himself as an invaluable member of Bobby Robson's squad. The introduction of Peter Beardsley helped to restore England's flagging reputation on the world stage. England were on their way out of the competition and discussing flight times home when Robson changed his team and gave Beardsley a chance in the starting line up against Poland.

England hadn't scored against Portugal or Morocco, but with Peter in the side, they suddenly found the net in dramatic fashion. They beat Poland 3–0, Lineker hitting all three, then Lineker scored two in the 3–0 win over Paraguay (Beardsley scored the other one) and one in the defeat by Argentina. At the end of the World Cup Lineker was the competition's top marksman but generously — and quite rightly — passed much of the credit for his goals to the running and creative ability of his new striking partner, Beardsley.

Peter returned from Mexico as one of the most sought-after strikers in the game. He spent a final season at Newcastle, scoring just five goals in a long hard struggle to stay in Division One, but it was becoming increasingly obvious that Newcastle would eventually sell him and in the summer of 1987 he moved to Liverpool. The Anfield club payed a record £1.9 million for his signature — it was a move that was sure to enhance Peter's goalscoring

England's Peter Beardsley races away against Northern Ireland in 1987. A late developer, he established an international reputation in the 1986 World Cup.

rate and, in his first season, he played a major role in helping Liverpool to win the First Division title.

He has so many of the qualities of a top class striker; he works hard, he tackles back deep into his own half, he's brave and he's not a striker who loses the ball and then allows his head to drop. But to be ranked among the world's top strikers he will have to increase his goalscoring rate. He has so many of Kevin Keegan's qualities but the one he doesn't have is the finishing instinct in the 18-yard box.

Like his Liverpool colleague, John Barnes, Beardsley looked tired during the 1988 European Championships. His performances against the Republic of Ireland and Holland were two of his most disappointing since he joined the England side, but I still feel that Peter has a key role to play in the build-up to the 1990 World Cup.

COLIN BELL

Colin Bell (midfield)
Heselden 26.2.46
Bury, Manchester City
England – 48

At Manchester City they called Colin Bell 'Nijinsky' after the racehorse and with very good reason. He was one of the fittest and most athletic players I came across and it was supremely ironic that his career should have been curtailed by a knee injury. He had genuine all-round ability with no significant weakness in his game. He could win the ball, use it well and score goals, but the most impressive aspect of his game was his tremendous running ability which was the reason for his nickname.

His career began with Horden Colliery Welfare where his potential was spotted by Bury. He scored 25 goals in 100 games for Bury between 1963 and 1965 before Manchester City paid a then club record fee of £45,000 for him. He became the midfield mastermind of the thrusting, young City side, coached by Malcolm Allison, that won the First Division title, FA Cup, European Cup-winners' Cup and League Cup in a four year spell in the late 1960s and early 1970s.

For a midfield player whose prodigious running was his prime quality, he was also an outstanding finisher. He played in over 400 games for City scoring more than 100 goals. He would have scored many more and made more than 49 appearances for England had it not been for a serious knee injury that brought his career to a premature end in 1978.

He made his England debut in 1968 but it wasn't until after the 1970 World Cup that he began to establish himself in Sir Alf Ramsey's team. I will always remember his outstanding contribution in that infamous World Cup qualifying tie against Poland at Wembley in 1973. By this time he had effectively taken Alan Ball's place in the side but, for all his running and enduring commitment over the 90 minutes, he could not prevent the Poles from securing the draw that earned them a World Cup place at England's expense. Bell was particularly disappointed: he never again had the chance to test himself against the best in the world.

I played against Colin when he was in the City forward line that included players like Rodney Marsh, Francis Lee and Mike Summerbee but it wasn't until I was called into the England squad that I got to know him. He was a super guy and always had time to speak to people. When I was a youngster coming into the side he made me feel very much at home among the big names of the game. Most young players joining the England squad for the first time find the experience a little daunting. Suddenly they are confronted with the biggest, most famous names in the sport and it can be an ordeal at first. I think Colin was aware that newcomers to the squad felt a little self-conscious and, as a youngster then myself, I can remember being reluctant to start conversations with the star names. But, if Colin was around, he would invariably draw you into the conversation.

I felt sorry for him when he had to retire because he was one of those naturally fit players who could have gone on for years in the way Billy Bonds did.

OPPOSITE *Colin Bell was a model professional as well as a nice person. His balance and athleticism earned him the nickname 'Nijinsky'.*

GEORGE BEST

George had one of the greatest individual talents, if not the greatest, since the war. It was a pleasure and privilege to play against him. Unfortunately, that was in the early years of my career and just as I was becoming established George decided to depart from the scene. He quit Manchester United when he was 27 with his best years still to come, in my opinion. I found the five years between 27 and 32 to be the most productive in my career and I often wonder whether George regrets leaving Old Trafford when he was so young. He flitted around with Stockport County, Fulham and Los Angeles Aztecs, but he wasn't the George Best we had admired so much in the red shirt of United.

At the age at which George left, a player has gathered the experience to maximise his ability and confidence. In a sense the public was cheated because we will never know how great he could have become, but I feel that he was capable of reaching Pele's status in the world. Best was one of those rare players who generated excitement whenever he got the ball. Even playing against him, with your concentration focused intently on the game, you could sense a buzz around the crowd when he had the ball because people expected something out of the ordinary from him.

George had fantastic dribbling ability; he could go past defenders with such ease that it was enthralling to watch. He had a natural ability and he was one of the most gifted footballers you could wish to see; his right and left foot were equally lethal and he could glide past defenders on either side. He had tremendous speed, great awareness and, although he was recognized as a winger, I saw him play down the middle as though he had been doing it all his career. At times he would over-elaborate when in possession, but he usually gave the simple pass, which is the most effective. He was strong and brave – in fact, the complete all-round forward.

I remember playing against him in September 1971 – the season that I established myself in the West Ham first team – and George scored a hat trick. We were having an early season run of success and felt unusually confident for a game at Old Trafford. They had all their stars, Charlton, Law, Stepney, Morgan etc., but on the day the man who beat us was George. United won 4–2 – I got a goal myself, that's probably why I remember the match so well! – and George ran all over us. I remember him taking a short corner, receiving a return pass, dribbling past three defenders and finally selling Bobby Moore a peach of a dummy before blasting the ball into the net. He was irresistible that day and it was a fantastic goal from a fantastic player. It was a shame that he never played in the World Cup with Northern Ireland because success on that stage would have enhanced his name worldwide.

George made his international debut a month short of his eighteenth birthday and probably reached the peak of his career in 1968 when he picked up the English and European Footballer of the Year awards after

George Best (winger)
Belfast 22.5.46
Manchester United, Stockport County, Fulham, Hibernian
Northern Ireland – 37

OPPOSITE *A rebel, a hero and an undisputed genius, George Best has gone down in history as one of world football's all-time greats.*

winning a European Cup-winners' medal to go with two League title medals. Unfortunately, George's brilliant career ended before it should have done largely because his behaviour off the field often let him down. He was constantly in the headlines for skipping training or disappearing from Old Trafford for days on end. In many ways he was his own worst enemy because there must have been people at Old Trafford trying to persuade him to lead a more conventional life. It seemed to me then that people were always making excuses for him. Eventually, the club lost patience with George and he lost credibility.

George was a rebel and everyone loves a rebel — look at McEnroe in tennis or Higgins in snooker. He was a flag carrier for a generation at a very exciting time in football. People love to see rebels do well; the media builds them up and then knocks them down, and the public loves to see them bounce back. But then the day comes when they don't bounce back. For all his faults he was a wonderful player and you have to say that he was good for the game. He was an entertainer — the sort of player that drew the fans through the turnstiles.

DANNY BLANCHFLOWER

I think Danny must have been one of the biggest influences on all the young players who were around when I was kicking a ball in the school playground. He was one of the big names of the early 1960s and a crucial member of the Spurs side that became the first this century to win the fabled League and FA Cup double. I was in my early teens when Spurs were at their peak and the name of Danny Blanchflower was synonymous with skill and good passing ability. He was a very polished and elegant performer – one of those players who always seemed to have time on the ball. Primarily right footed and not renowned for his tackling, he was a touch player who provided the creative momentum in Tottenham's assault on the double.

In the playground kickabouts everyone wanted to be Danny Blanchflower. He was, of course, captain of the most successful and glamorous team of the time and the media acknowledged him to be an outstanding exponent of the game. He was a high-profile player: I used to watch him

Danny Blanchflower (midfield)
Belfast 10.2.26
Glentoran, Barnsley, Aston
Villa, Tottenham Hotspur
Northern Ireland – 56

Danny Blanchflower (left), a
polished and elegant performer,
parades the FA Cup with Bobby
Smith and his double-winning
Tottenham team-mates in 1961.

a lot and it amazed me how often he was in possession of the ball. When you saw the accuracy of his passing it was easy to understand why Spurs channelled most of their attacking moves through him. It was an education to watch him in action.

Danny began his career with Glentoran in Northern Ireland before joining Barnsley in 1949. He spent two years in Yorkshire and then four years with Aston Villa where he established himself in the Northern Ireland side. He joined Spurs for £30,000 in 1954, winning the recognition his talents deserved. He was a fine, constructive wing half in the classic mould who had a wonderful ability to run the game. One of the secrets of successful midfield play is availability and Danny constantly wanted the ball. He was always ready to receive the ball from his defence and to support his forwards and he was rarely far from the action.

'Danny Boy' captained Ireland through to the last eight of the World Cup in 1958, for which he received the Footballer of the Year award. He won it again three years later when Spurs achieved the double and remains one of the few players who have won the trophy twice. In total he won 56 caps for Northern Ireland and with today's international schedules he would have been fairly sure of making 100 appearances. If he had a failing it was that he didn't score goals – only 27 in around 600 games at club level – but his passing and leadership qualities more than compensated for that.

He had a younger brother, Jackie, who was a centre half with Manchester United and Northern Ireland but he was injured in the Munich air disaster and didn't play again. Danny retired from the game in 1964 and began a successful career in journalism. These days I see him most often at golfing events where his handicap frequently gives him an opportunity to feature among the prizes.

BILLY BONDS

I have no doubt that Billy Bonds was one of the best all-round players of my generation. The aggression of his play was an element that was frequently highlighted and there's no doubt that in his early years he had one or two clashes with referees and accumulated more disciplinary points than he should have done. This aspect of his play earned him a 'hard man' reputation that probably overshadowed his many other qualities as a player. He was a super passer of the ball, had tremendous awareness and could use both feet. What made him so valuable to West Ham was his versatility. He joined the club from Charlton as a lean, young right back, moved into midfield and finished his career at centre back. I think I most appreciated him in midfield where he became my 'minder' for seven or eight years.

If anyone kicked me during a game I used to give Bill a wink and say 'Bonzo! Have you seen what he's doing to me?' Then Bill would sort them out in the next five minutes and I'd have the freedom of the midfield for the rest of the game. When he was playing in the back four he got called up by England on two or three occasions. In May 1981 Ron Greenwood, who was then the England manager, called him into the squad with the intention of playing him alongside Alvin Martin against Brazil. Then on the eve of the FA Cup final Bill cracked two ribs in a game against Sheffield Wednesday and he lost his chance. If he could have got into the side at that time – about 14 months before the 1982 World Cup – I think he would have stayed in it. He was the best captain I played under. Bobby Moore led by example but Bill encouraged the players in a way that really brought the best out of us. He was a dominant, inspiring figure on the field, but very shy off it. I think if he had projected himself more he would have captained the national side.

I've always felt that the players who get in the newspapers a great deal are the ones who often enjoy the benefits of such promotion: they get talked about a lot, managers are more aware of them and that inevitably enhances their chances of recognition at international level. But Bill was never greedy for publicity. He was always happy to keep a low profile. After a home match at Upton Park he would be first out of the dressing room and on his way home before the press had begun to gather for the after-match briefings. An incident before the 1980 FA Cup final against Arsenal illustrates his attitude to publicity.

The team was staying at a hotel in Hendon on the afternoon before the game and we were told that the television cameras were coming to film us. I was sharing a room with Bill and just before the television people were due he decided to 'pop down to the betting shop for five minutes'. He stayed there for three and a half hours and returned assuming that he had missed the television interviews. You can imagine his horror when he discovered that because of technical hitches the recording had been put back to that evening. He agreed to co-operate only as long as he could sit

Billy Bonds MBE (midfield)
Woolwich 17.9.46
Charlton Athletic, West Ham United

in the background and the interviewer didn't ask him any questions. As captain of the team he was often asked for interviews and he would invariably say to me, 'I don't want to do this. Will you do it for me?' We were like chalk and cheese yet we became very close personal friends. I could tell him anything and know it wouldn't go any further.

Billy is a family man who enjoys country walks and bird watching. Now and again when we were zooming along the motorway in the team bus he'd suddenly spot a bird hovering over a field and declare 'Oh! That's a so and so.' His fitness, of course, is legendary – he put the rest of us to shame. In pre-season runs he'd stay with me for the first mile, smile sympathetically and then say, 'I'd better start moving up a bit now'. By the time I'd finished Billy would have had his shower and be on his way home. He won the cross-country race for 18 seasons on the trot.

Bill was great fun and if he had one failing it was that he was not a good communicator. Nowadays he's coaching at West Ham and if he can develop his communication skills he will become as good a coach as he was a player. Quite amazingly, in 1987–88 he was recalled to the first team at the age of 41. He was still playing like a youngster and someone was obviously impressed because I awoke one morning to read in the newspapers that he had deservedly been awarded the MBE for services to football.

OPPOSITE *At an age when most other men are relaxing in their armchairs, West Ham's Billy Bonds was proving that there is life after 40!*

STAN BOWLES

Stan Bowles (striker)
Manchester 24.12.48
Manchester City, Bury, Crewe
Alexandra, Carlisle United,
Queen's Park Rangers,
Nottingham Forest, Orient,
Brentford
England − 5

Stan was one of the great characters in the game during my time as a player but, sadly, he often got into the headlines for all the wrong reasons. He was a gambler and every now and then his liking for a bet would introduce some fresh crisis into his life. Had he been an ordinary man in the street no one would have been interested, but because he was a professional footballer, and a very gifted one at that, he became a very newsworthy person. This newspaper coverage of his private life inevitably gave him a rebellious image which was unfortunate because he was a wonderful player and, in my experience, a very amiable, easy going guy.

If his attitude had been a little more mature I feel he would have achieved far greater distinction in the game. He was born in Manchester and started promisingly enough with City at Maine Road but then disappeared from the big time for nearly three years when he played for Bury, Crewe and Carlisle. I think this spell in the lower divisions was probably a reflection on Stan as a person rather than on Stan as a player because in 1972 Gordon Jago, then manager of QPR, decided to take a risk with him and brought him to Loftus Road where his talent finally blossomed.

I think Jago was a good influence on Stan and he should be grateful for the chance Jago gave him. Had he signed for another club where attitudes were a little less strict he might never have gone on to play for England. As it was, Stan was signed to replace the charismatic Rodney Marsh and was soon establishing himself as a worthy successor to the clown prince of Loftus Road. He quickly struck up a rapport with the fans similar to that which Rodney had enjoyed.

There were few players who could follow Rodney at Rangers, but Stan was one of them. He was an entertainer with a great left foot; he had good tight control, good dribbling skills and he liked to chip and curl his shots at the goal. But he wasn't the quickest of strikers and that's probably why he played only five times for England. His deft touch and dribbling ability would get him past defenders but he didn't have the pace to accelerate towards the goal.

I played alongside Stan in a crucial World Cup qualifying tie in Italy in 1976 towards the end of the Don Revie reign as England manager. A lot was expected of Stan but he failed to produce the goods. I don't think he ever really came to terms with the man-to-man marking and the body checking that goes on in international football at that level.

I think he was one of those lads who simply enjoyed playing football for the sake of it. He would probably have played on a park pitch three times at weekends had he not become a professional. But he had a wonderful talent that deserved the big showman's stage of the First Division every Saturday afternoon. His best years were at Rangers where he played in 255 League games, scoring 70 goals.

In 1979 Brian Clough signed him for Nottingham Forest but he was there for only a few months, playing just 19 League games before moving on to Orient. He ended his career at Brentford and, for a player who provided so much entertainment for so many people, it saddens me to think that he left the game with so little. In 1987 his domestic life was still in some turmoil and I was delighted when Brentford staged a testimonial match for him. The testimonial committee invested the proceeds of the game in a trust to ensure that Stan had a regular income. He was the sort who made a lot of friends in the game and it's nice to think that some of them were prepared to help him when his great days were over.

One of the most talented left-footed attacking players of the 1970s, Stan Bowles enjoyed his best season with Queen's Park Rangers.

BILLY BREMNER

There's no doubt in my mind that Billy Bremner and Johnny Giles formed one of the most formidable midfield partnerships in the game during Don Revie's reign as manager of Leeds United. Neither player looked particularly impressive size-wise but few could match them for effort, aggression and skill. Small, Scotch and ginger, Bremner was a fiery little competitor who had an aggressive streak that got him into trouble with referees and other players. I well remember the clash he had with Kevin Keegan when Leeds met Liverpool during the 1974 Charity Shield at Wembley. After Bremner and Keegan were sent off both players removed their shirts – an act that did little for the image of the game on what was supposed to be a charitable occasion. As a result they received unprecedented punishment – both were fined £500 and their suspensions meant that each missed 11 matches.

Bremner's volatile temperament seemed to fuel a human dynamo of a body that was prepared to run for 90 minutes and cover every inch of the pitch. He made his debut as a 17-year-old left winger alongside Revie in 1960. Later, as captain, he was the man who ensured that the manager's instructions were carried out on the field. In many ways he epitomised the Leeds spirit of that time. He hated losing and between 1965 and 1975 rarely finished on the losing side. His collection of honours includes two League titles, an FA Cup-winners' medal and a Fairs Cup-winners' medal. When Leeds did lose, though, defeat could be significant and Bremner finished on the losing side three times in four FA Cup finals.

The Leeds team of the time was frequently criticised for 'professionalism' – a word used to describe their time wasting tactics. But, to their credit, they were a very accomplished team – Revie's astute signings meant that he could field a team comprising 11 full internationals.

Bremner was primarily a right footed player whom I thought was particularly good at covering his own defenders. He had a crisp, no-nonsense tackle, but also the skill to set up attacks with a quick pass. The passing ability of Bremner and Giles helped Leeds to perfect their possession game. They were always reluctant to give the ball away and were one of the first teams to play possession football. Bremner was particularly good at hitting a square pass across his body with his right foot while in full stride.

Because of Leeds' mean streak and Bremner's own aggression, he was never high on the popularity list among opposing supporters but everyone in the game recognised the contribution he made to Leeds United's success. He was voted Footballer of the Year in 1970, when Leeds were runners-up in both the League championship and FA Cup, and in a distinguished international career won 54 Scottish caps. When he retired as a player he took the same commitment into management. He led Doncaster Rovers out of Division Four in 1981 and five years later returned to Leeds as manager, just missing out on promotion to Division One in 1986–87.

Billy Bremner (midfield)
Stirling 9.12.42
Leeds United, Hull City,
Doncaster Rovers
Scotland – 54

OPPOSITE *Billy Bremner, the human dynamo. The smile on the face of the tiger disguises a volatile temperament.*

PETER BROADBENT

Peter Broadbent (midfield)
Ellerington 15.5.33
Brentford, Wolverhampton
Wanderers, Shrewsbury Town,
Aston Villa, Stockport County
England – 7

During the months I took pondering over my 100 players for this book I happened to talk with a lifelong Wolves supporter who used to watch Peter Broadbent regularly. I told him that I had been a fan of Peter and was thinking of including him in my book. 'A great choice', the Wolves fan enthused. 'He was brilliant. No player at the club has given me more pleasure.'

I can remember watching Peter when I was a youngster and thinking how stylish and elegant he looked. I remember him best as a Wolves player, but by the time he retired in 1969 his distinguished career had taken in a handful of clubs – Brentford, Wolves, Shrewsbury, Aston Villa and Stockport County – and, of course, England. He had been a brilliant teenager playing for his home town club, Dover, when Brentford snapped him up as a 16-year-old in 1950. He joined the club at the same time as Ron Greenwood, my former manager at West Ham and England. When I asked him about Peter, he likened his playing style to that of my own. Ron told me that Peter always had time on the ball, even as a young player. 'That was because of his good control', he explained. 'But passing was his greatest strength. He didn't score a lot of goals, but his passing meant that he created a lot for other people'.

Peter played only 16 games for Brentford before the mighty Wolves, one of the great clubs of the time, signed him for £10,000 on the advice of George Poyser, who had discovered him earlier. A tall, elegant, thoughtful inside forward, it was almost inevitable that Peter would flourish in the glamorous Wolves side of the time. In 15 years there he became one of their most influential players, playing in three League title winning sides and in the team that beat Blackburn Rovers in the 1960 FA Cup final. What struck me most about him was the accuracy of his passing. He was primarily right footed, but could strike the ball with the inside and outside of his foot. He was more of a push and run player, than a speculative long passer, but he was always very creative, very positive and saw opportunities early.

There were a number of players that I enjoyed watching in those days, but few gave me more pleasure than Peter Broadbent. He had quite an influence on my own development as a player, and he wore the number 10 shirt, too! Had there not been so many good players in the England squad at the time Peter was at his peak, I'm sure he would have won far more than seven caps. He made his debut against the USSR in 1958 – his club captain Billy Wright led the side – but was competing for places in a forward line with players like Jimmy Greaves, Johnny Haynes and Bobby Charlton. In 453 games for Wolves he scored 127 goals before moving to Shrewsbury in 1965. After two years he played briefly for Aston Villa and finished his career with a handful of games for Stockport County in 1969.

OPPOSITE *Peter Broadbent*
represents England against
Scotland in 1959. An
accomplished passer, he was
unfortunately at his peak during
an era of great inside forwards,
which restricted his international
career.

TERRY BUTCHER

Terry Butcher (centre back)
Singapore 28.12.58
Ipswich Town, Glasgow
Rangers
England – 54

One of England's great centre backs, Terry Butcher, tangles with the Republic of Ireland's Eamonn O'Keefe in 1985. Injury kept Butcher out of the 1988 European Championships: he was sorely missed.

It's a cliché I know, but Terry is one of the game's gentle giants; he is 6 ft 3 in and was born in Singapore where his father was in the services. He's a very popular lad within the profession, always finds time to talk to people, and was considered an outstanding ambassador for the game. I say 'was' only because his image was somewhat tarnished when he became one of three players to be sent off in the Glasgow Rangers–Celtic game in 1987.

What the public probably doesn't realise is just how competitive Terry is. I've always considered him to be a very strong but fair opponent yet he goes through a routine of psyching himself up that I found quite alarming when I first experienced it in the England dressing room. He's tremendous for team spirit because he strides around the dressing room before a match shouting at himself and others. 'Come on, we're going to beat this lot', is usually the tone of his team talk. Just before we walk onto the pitch he releases a huge elephant-like bellow as if to say, 'come on, wake up you lot. We're going out now.'

Terry made his debut for Ipswich in 1977 and soon formed a very sound defensive partnership with Russell Osman. Terry and Russell were an important part of a very fine side built by Bobby Robson with players like the two Dutch lads Frans Thijssen and Arnold Muhren and Mick Mills and Paul Mariner. Terry was a promising player in those days but I wondered whether he had the mobility to become an international class defender.

He was tall and as strong as a bull and as the Ipswich side developed he developed with it. Today I think he must be one of the most accomplished centre backs in the world and one of England's most consistent and reliable performers. He was outstanding in my last international tournament – the 1982 World Cup in Spain.

Terry has become more than just a giant stopper. He has a very good left foot and can use the ball to excellent effect. In fact, his distribution has become one of the strong points of his game. Strikers might edge in front of him over the first few yards but he is deceptively quick and his long legs usually put him within tackling range in a few strides. Occasionally, in very tight situations, he gets turned by a striker but it's rare to see him exposed.

Of course, he is a dominant figure in the air and is always getting on the end of corners and free kicks. Like many good defenders he sometimes shows a complete disregard for his own safety and one collision produced a nose bleed from which he lost so much blood that he almost died.

I was surprised when he chose to join Glasgow Rangers in 1986 when several English clubs like Spurs and Manchester United were strongly tipped to get him, but he chose Scottish football and has no regrets. He is now idolised in Glasgow and his defensive partnership with former Spurs defender, Graham Roberts, played a crucial role in Rangers' championship triumph in 1986–87.

I think Terry showed great loyalty to Ipswich when a number of top players were leaving the club; he was devoted to Portman Road and even when Robson left to become England manager, Terry stayed. However, when Ipswich were relegated to Division Two I think Terry felt that he had no choice but to leave if he wanted to maintain his standing as a defender of international class.

Although fiercely competitive by nature, his much-publicised sending-off was entirely out of character. The incident has to be put in context because the Celtic–Rangers games in Glasgow are traditionally volatile, which was something the police were probably very conscious of when they decided to prosecute for breach of the peace. His initial offence was to push away Celtic's former West Ham striker Frank McAvennie when he rushed into the Rangers goalkeeper Chris Woods, with Graham Roberts later joining the affray. When McAvennie crumpled to the pitch both sets of supporters were in an ugly mood. Woods and McAvennie were sent off and Butcher only cautioned, but a later foul on Celtic's Allen McKnight, the Northern Ireland goalkeeper, resulted in the big centre half following the other two to the dressing room. Six months later, in April 1988, in a decision which could have far reaching consequences for sport, Terry was fined £250, and Chris Woods £500, in Glasgow Sheriff Court. McAvennie was acquitted and the case against Roberts was not proven. The immediate speculation that Butcher, Woods and Roberts would leave Scottish football was silenced at a press conference a few days after the court case, but Roberts left at the end of the season after differences with Souness.

Terry, though, signed a one-year extension to his contract, committing himself to Rangers for a further three years in total. Apart from the worry of the court case, Terry was fighting a personal battle to recover from a broken leg – sustained against Aberdeen in November 1987 – in time to play for England in the 1988 European Championships. He finally gave up the fight at the end of the Scottish season. It was, perhaps, the biggest worry for England manager Bobby Robson because, at his best, Terry is an irreplaceable defender and an outstandingly good influence on the team.

JOHNNY BYRNE

Everyone at West Ham knew Johnny Byrne as 'Budgie' because he never stopped talking – on or off the field. He had a bubbly, extrovert personality and was a wonderful player who had a big influence on my early development. As a young supporter of West Ham I looked forward every week to watching Budgie because he would always do something that got me up out of my seat. He was one of those players who never hid, even when he was going through a bad spell he was always looking for the ball.

He liked to lace his game with little tricks and one of the most spectacular features of his play was the way he would stand with his back to the goal and volley a long first time pass to our wide men, John Sissons on the left and Peter Brabrook on the right. His vision, little twists, and one–twos, really were a joy to watch and he was a great encouragement to young players. I always left after a game thinking, 'Cor! The way he did that was good. I must try it when I get home.'

Johnny was still playing at Upton Park when I joined the club and I was immediately struck by his sense of humour – he loved mickey-taking and joking with the youngsters. He always had time for a chat and he liked to pass on little hints. Off the field he enjoyed himself and he didn't always lead the life a professional should. That was John and you had to warm to him because of his character. There are several players among my 100 who were extremely talented on the field but a lack of dedication to their profession in their everyday lives meant they never quite fulfilled their potential as players. I think John probably comes into that category.

John won his first England cap playing Third Division soccer with Crystal Palace and after being transferred to West Ham for a then record fee of £58,000 plus a player it looked as though he could do no wrong. He was ready-made for West Ham because he was the sort of player who loved the quick passing game that the Upton Park manager at the time, Ron Greenwood, advocated. John was in West Ham's FA Cup winning team against Preston in 1964, but won only 11 England caps when he should have won far more. He was particularly dangerous in front of the goal, having the skill to manoeuvre a shooting chance in a tight space. He scored eight goals for England, but that wasn't enough to win him a regular place. However, there is no doubt that Budgie's influence and direction on the field helped Geoff Hurst to make the transition from being an average wing half to being a striker feared throughout the world. John went back to Palace in 1967 and, after just one season, finished his career with Fulham.

I don't think anyone could dispute that John had the ability to be a regular member of the England side, but there were a number of other contenders for the attacking positions in the team at that time. That apart, Alf Ramsey set great store by the smooth performance of the team as a unit and this left little room for improvisation. John was basically an individualist, and Alf's system allowed for no such unpredictability.

Johnny Byrne (striker)
West Horsley 13.5.39
Crystal Palace, West Ham
United, Fulham
England – 11

IAN CALLAGHAN

Ian Callaghan MBE (midfield)
Liverpool 10.4.42
Liverpool, Swansea City
England – 4

Ian was one of the old fashioned wingers who found he had to adapt his style when Sir Alf Ramsey's success with 4–4–2 changed the winger's role. He had been a right winger, but Liverpool turned him into a central midfield player – and a very successful and exciting one he became, too. His appetite for the ball and his work-rate became essential elements in the development of the Bill Shankly side that laid the foundations for Liverpool's long domination of the domestic game.

Ian was one of the most consistent players of my era and you could always guarantee when you played against Liverpool that 'Cally' would give a totally committed performance for the full 90 minutes. He wasn't one of those players who grabbed the headlines but if you played against him regularly and talked with the Liverpool players about him you soon realised why he was held in such high esteem at Anfield. His winger's instincts meant that he could run with the ball and wriggle away from defenders and he was a very neat and positive influence on the Liverpool midfield during those formative years under Shankly.

He was one of the gentlemen of the game and meeting him off the field one might have felt that he lacked the natural aggression to survive in the frenzied battleground of the midfield. He was a determined yet fair and sporting competitor and was rarely cautioned by referees. He joined Liverpool in 1960 and in an 18-year career made 640 League appearances, an Anfield record. He played in five championship winning teams and picked up winners' medals in the FA Cup (twice), the European Cup (twice) and the UEFA Cup. He was also voted Footballer of the Year in 1974.

Ian played only four times for England, which was scant reward for an outstanding club career. He would probably have won only two caps had it not been for Ron Greenwood's decision to recall him to the international scene. Cally made his first two appearances in 1966 playing in a World Cup warm-up against Finland and later in the tournament itself against France. Sir Alf Ramsey didn't consider him again but 11 years later Greenwood decided to try a block of Liverpool players in a friendly match against Switzerland at Wembley.

He chose Ray Clemence, Phil Neal, Emlyn Hughes, Terry McDermott, Ray Kennedy, Kevin Keegan, who had not long left Liverpool for Hamburg, and Callaghan, who by this time was 35. Cally gave a steady performance in a goalless draw and retained his place for the next match, a 2–0 win in Luxembourg. The fact that he was even considered for international football at that age speaks volumes for his durability. He finally left Liverpool in 1978 and went to Swansea where he helped his old team-mate John Toshack to lift the Welsh side out of the Third Division.

LEFT *A busy, darting midfield player, Ian Callaghan enjoyed an unblemished career with Liverpool, Swansea and England.*

MIKE CHANNON

Mike Channon (striker)
Orcheston 28.11.48
Southampton, Manchester
City, Newcastle United, Bristol
Rovers, Norwich City,
Portsmouth
England – 46

I think Micky Channon was one of the most confident players I ever met. He lacked nothing in self-assurance and had total belief in his own ability. He knew his strengths and did everything he could to maximise them. I first came across him on an England youth trip and can remember being impressed by his ability on the ball and by his confidence. It was obvious in the mid-1960s that he was a player with a great future ahead of him.

Mick's skills were beyond dispute. Throughout my career I saw players who looked electric on the training pitch but didn't always perform to their potential in front of big crowds in match situations. Mick's tenacity never wavered. He always achieved a consistently high level of play whether it was for England or merely in a training game. Even in those games when things were not going well for him, his commitment was relentless. There are days when some attacking players simply put their hands in the air and declare: 'The defender is just too good for me'. But Mick would still be running at defenders, trying to get behind them, in the 90th minute, even if the previous 89 minutes had been fruitless and frustrating. He always had a belief that at some stage during a game he would do something that would have an effect on the result.

He worked his way through the Southampton youth ranks and made his first team debut at Easter in 1966, but it wasn't until 1967–68 that he began to establish himself in the side. He eventually formed an exciting attacking partnership with the Wales striker, Ron Davies, whose heading ability complemented perfectly Channon's work on the ground. Micky was a powerful runner who loved to take on defenders and, when in full stride, he could be an exhilarating sight. He was primarily right footed, but he could use the inside or outside of the foot and this meant that he wasn't restricted when facing a defender.

Cutting inside or outside a marker, Micky's pace would usually carry him clear of trouble though, inevitably for such a quick player, he was frequently the victim of some heavy challenges, but he was a dogged competitor with the temperament to handle the most intimidating opposition. I think his effervescent personality probably played a role in lifting the spirits of team-mates when a game wasn't going to plan. He had good close control and, apart from setting up chances for team-mates like Davies, created many goalscoring opportunities for himself.

If I have a criticism of him it is that his finishing sometimes lets him down. He made good openings for himself but was too often careless in front of the goal. Even so, he scored 182 League goals – a club record – in 15 seasons with Southampton. The highlight of those years must have been in 1976 when Southampton, then in the Second Division, beat Manchester United 1–0 with a Bobby Stokes goal in the FA Cup final at Wembley. By this time Micky was an established England striker and was forming an attacking partnership at Southampton with Peter Osgood.

Micky won a total of 46 England caps, scoring 21 goals — a far higher goalscoring ratio than he managed at club level. I know Micky felt a little aggrieved that his international career finished much earlier than he had anticipated. He made his debut with England under Sir Alf Ramsey in 1972 and was a regular during Don Revie's reign as manager. He played in Ron Greenwood's first game against Switzerland in September 1977, was substituted and never selected again. He was then 28 and just starting a two year spell at Manchester City. In 1979 he returned to the Dell and spent three more years there before moving to Newcastle United for a short time.

He then moved to Bristol Rovers and Norwich City and at the age of 37 was still playing at Portsmouth, managed by his former Southampton team-mate, Alan Ball. His legs were going a little by this time, but in 1986–87 Alan would send him on for an hour and let him rip before replacing him with fresher legs. Mick was a horseracing fan and one of the attractions of retirement was that he would be able to spend more time at the stables and on the courses.

The FA Charity Shield 1976: the ever-confident Mike Channon in attack for Southampton, the club where he produced his most effective football.

55

JOHN CHARLES

John Charles (striker)
Swansea 27.12.31
Leeds United, Juventus, Roma,
Cardiff City
Wales – 38

Ask a Welshman to name the finest footballer who ever lived and the chances are that he'll reply John Charles. By any standards, Charles was a player of exceptional talent and certainly one of the best ever to pull on the red shirt of Wales. He came from Swansea and when I was a schoolboy he was one of the biggest personalities in the game and one of my favourite footballers, not just because of his skill but because of his £65,000 transfer from Leeds to Juventus in Italy. To a schoolboy in the 1950s that was an unimaginable amount of money. For that sort of money he had to be brilliant at shooting, heading, attacking and defending. The fact is, he was brilliant at everything. The only argument about him in the school playground concerned his role in the game. Was he the world's best centre half, or the world's best centre forward? I think it is a debate that will never be resolved. My own view is that the goals he scored make him primarily a striker of outstanding quality. In today's transfer market his goalscoring prowess would boost his value considerably more than would his defensive attributes, and, quite apart from that, I'm sure the modern coach would be more interested in exploiting his attacking potential rather than playing him at centre half.

The first and perhaps still the most successful footballing export to the Continent, John Charles, makes an instant impression at Turin airport as he arrives to sign for Juventus.

John Charles was a huge, exceptionally talented player with the lightest of touches on the ball and a gentle and chivalrous temperament. He spent a few months with his local club, Swansea, but by his seventeenth birthday had been enticed by Major Frank Buckley to sign for Leeds United, then

in the Second Division. At 18 he was playing the first of his 38 internationals for Wales. In those early days he was a 6 ft 2 in centre half with a powerful tackle, sure control and polished distribution. But in the 1952–53 season Leeds experimented with him at centre forward. He scored 27 goals in 30 games and the following season he was the Football League's top marksman with 42 goals which is still a club record. In 1956 Charles helped Leeds to win promotion and in their first season in the big time he finished the top scorer in Division One with 38 goals.

The following year the prestigious Italian club, Juventus, backed by the Fiat car fortune, bid £65,000 for Charles. It was a British record transfer fee and Leeds quickly agreed to release him and so he became the first British player to move to Italy. The Italians loved him. He achieved superstar status overnight in Turin where they called him 'Il Gigante Buono'. They admired his authority in the air, his sportsmanship, his bravery and his skill on the ball. To this day he is remembered affectionately in Turin and the arrival in the city of another Welshman, Ian Rush, prompted many nostalgic pieces in the Italian newspapers about Charles.

John spent five happy years with Juventus, helping them to win the League title three times and the Cup twice. He scored nearly 100 goals in a country where defence was a way of life. They never really discovered his best position, but they compromised – they would send him out as a centre forward and when he had scored they would pull him back to centre half to protect the lead. I can't think of another player who could fulfill both roles with equal ease. His height and powerful build – he had a thick neck like a heavyweight boxer – made him a natural centre half, but his shooting, his touch on the ball and his strong running made him equally effective at centre forward. Charles considered the defensive job to be the easier of the two.

He spent a short time at Leeds in 1962 but after a few months went back to Italy with Roma for £70,000. In 1963 he returned to his native Wales, ending his career with two seasons at Cardiff, playing alongside his younger brother Mel. Since my schooldays I've come to realise just how remarkable and talented a player John Charles was in his 17-year career. I would go so far as to say that he was unique.

BOBBY CHARLTON

*Bobby Charlton CBE
(midfield)
Ashington 11.10.37
Manchester United, Preston
North End
England – 106*

Bobby Charlton was at one time probably the best known English footballer in the world. The fame he achieved was entirely justified because he was not only a marvellous player but also a wonderful ambassador for English sportsmanship. When I was a youngster there was no single player I particularly idolised but Bobby was the one I most enjoyed watching. For me he was an all-rounder of immense talent and fortitude. Like so many youngsters in the 1950s I think I took a close interest in his career largely because he was one of the survivors of the terrible air disaster at Munich in 1958. He was one of the young Lions in the team of 'Busby Babes' and I think a whole generation of kids grew up to look upon him as a symbol of all that was good in the English game.

He was from the famous Milburn footballing family in the North East and was a brilliant boy prodigy before going from England schoolboys to Old Trafford in the early 1950s. His older brother, Jack, was already with Leeds United. Bobby soon become famous for his terrific shooting ability and by the time the 1966 World Cup came round he was firmly established as everyone's favourite player. I think the stunning long range goal he scored against Mexico at Wembley in the finals was the launching pad for England's later success. The spectacular shot from the edge of the area was to become as much of a trademark as his thin flowing hair.

He often worked for his own openings, running from deep positions, striking a forward pass, taking the return in full stride before hitting a clubbing drive towards the goal. He was a scorer of great goals, rather than a great goalscorer, although he hit 49 for England in 106 appearances – a post-war record. Unlike many marksmen, he was more than willing to do his share of the donkey work in midfield and he was a prodigious chaser of lost causes. His cross-field passing was superb and he was one of the best strikers of a long ball I've seen.

Perhaps what set him apart as a personality – and this is something young players today would do well to remember – is that his conduct on and off the field was exemplary. Most dads when scolding their sons would say, 'Bobby Charlton wouldn't behave like that'. He was the epitomy of the sporting English gentleman – fair and honest but with an unshakeable determination to win and to battle against all the odds. His temperament inevitably brought him into conflict with George Best when George was going off the rails at Old Trafford. As personalities they were totally different but each was a crucial component in that wonderful Manchester United side that won the European Cup in 1968. When Bobby finally finished his career as player–manager at Preston he had a European Cup medal, and FA Cup-winners' medal, two League championship medals and he had also won the Footballer of the Year award. His services to the game were acknowledged with the CBE.

OPPOSITE Bobby Charlton, probably the most recognisable English footballer in the world. His immense reputation was enhanced by his ability to shoot and pass equally well with either foot.

JACK CHARLTON

Jack Charlton OBE (centre back)
Ashington 8.5.35
Leeds United .
England − 35

Jack is probably one of the most interesting personalities to have emerged in football since the war. As a player he was a late developer but he enjoyed enormous success with Leeds and worldwide fame in England's 1966 World Cup final triumph and then developed another career in television where his humour and northern bluntness made him a much sought-after celebrity. Not that Jack ever wanted to be a celebrity; he and younger brother, Bobby, came from the footballing Milburn family in the North East where men were men and pansies were things that grew in the park.

As a player, Jack was a genuinely hard man and not to be underestimated. He joined Leeds in 1952 and when John Charles moved to centre forward he took over at centre half and began to build himself an impressive reputation. All his early experience with Leeds was initially in the Second Division and it wasn't until 1964, just short of his thirtieth birthday, that he was selected to make his England debut against Scotland. He went on to play for England 35 times and was one of the most competitive performers in the 1966 World Cup.

A big, bluff, loveable Geordie, but on the field Jack Charlton was a hard man and certainly not to be underestimated.

Jack became a key figure in the success of Don Revie's Leeds side in the 1960s and 1970s and his long neck and ungainly style earned him the nickname 'The Giraffe'. He was 6 ft 2 in tall, a wiry and awkward opponent who may have lacked subtlety but made up for that with an uncompromising attitude. I'm sure that many strikers in those days must have thought that they would be able to run the legs off Jack, but that was rarely the case. Few opponents got the better of him. He was an intimidating defender with experience and a mean tackle.

He enjoyed football and he had a refreshing outlook on the game. He loved, and still does, fishing, shooting and spending time in the peace of the countryside. He always seemed to have his career under control; football wasn't the only thing that mattered in his life. Even later in his career, when he was manager of Middlesbrough, Sheffield Wednesday and Newcastle he found time to take himself off into the hills to enjoy the country life. It was typical of Jack that he should choose, as manager of the Republic of Ireland, to be holidaying on a beach in Spain when the rest of the European football community was in Düsseldorf for the 1988 European Championship draw. Under Charlton, the Republic of Ireland reached a major championship final for the first time – surely one of the most satisfying achievements of his managerial career – and were unfortunate not to reach the semi-finals.

Apart from the World Cup he also won the League championship, FA Cup, League Cup and Fairs Cup with Leeds but although Jack made a record 629 League appearances for Leeds all the glory and adulation came late in his career at an age when he could keep it in perspective. I think the fact that there was not an ounce of pretence about him, plus the fact that he could be quite blunt and outspoken, made him a very popular figure as a television pundit.

One unique feature of Jack's career is that he won the Footballer of the Year award in 1967, a year after his brother Bobby had won it – a family double that is unlikely to be repeated.

MARTIN CHIVERS

Martin Chivers (striker)
Southampton 27.4.45
Southampton, Tottenham
Hotspur, Servette, Norwich
City, Brighton and Hove
Albion
England — 24

Big Martin had all the attributes of a great striker but although he played 24 times for England I don't think he quite fulfilled his immense potential. He suffered with injuries but, even so, should have dominated the England centre forward role for far longer than three years. He was nearly 6 ft 2 in tall and had a powerful physique with coat hanger shoulders. In full flight he was an intimidating prospect for any defender; he had the classic build for a centre forward, but I feel he lacked the natural aggression to go with it. Nonetheless, he had a talent for goalscoring and from the moment he got into the Southampton side in 1962 he scored goals regularly throughout an 18-year career. He had scored 100 goals in 170 League games for Southampton when they decided to sell him to Tottenham Hotspur for £125,000 — a massive fee in 1968.

Martin spent eight years at White Hart Lane and although he seemed at times to have a love–hate relationship with the manager, Bill Nicholson, he was an outstanding success, overcoming a serious knee injury and establishing himself in the England side. No one could question his all-round ability in front of the goal but I suspect that Nicholson would have liked occasionally to see a few rough-house techniques from his big striker. At the time it was fashionable to argue that the only way to fully motivate Martin was to upset or anger him. Perhaps he took his responsibilities a little too casually. He was widely criticised for not using his strength to greater effect in that fateful 1973 game against Poland that cost England a place in the finals of the World Cup.

He scored 13 goals in his 24 England appearances and more than 100 in 270 League games with Spurs. He was capable of executing spectacular goals that brought the crowd out of their seats — one long range effort I particularly remember came in the first leg of the 1972 UEFA Cup final against Wolves. He was more noted, though, for his heading ability, timing his jumps superbly. I still play one or two charity games with him and his touch and finishing ability have survived the years quite well.

Alan Gilzean, a crafty Scot, provided Chivers with the perfect foil at Spurs. They worked together superbly, Gilzean frequently drifting to the near post where a glancing back-header would provide Chivers with the chance to climb above the opposing defence and get his head to the ball. They played together in Tottenham's two League Cup winning teams of 1971 and 1973. Martin scored both goals against Aston Villa in a 2–0 victory in the 1971 final. After leaving Spurs, Martin spent three successful years with Servette in Switzerland and returned to England to finish his career with Norwich and Brighton.

OPPOSITE *The powerfully-built Martin Chivers scored 13 goals for England in 24 appearances, but he sometimes failed to utilise his natural strength to the full.*

RAY CLEMENCE

*Ray Clemence MBE
(goalkeeper)
Skegness 5.8.48
Scunthorpe United, Liverpool,
Tottenham Hotspur
England – 61*

*A wonderful goalkeeper with a
keen sense of anticipation, Ray
Clemence was one of the first to
make a habit of leaving his
penalty area to cut out long
through balls.*

Ray was one of the finest goalkeepers in the history of the English game
and was simply unlucky to be around at the same time as Peter Shilton. If
only one of them had been in the game I think either Ray or Peter would
have been sure to surpass the goalkeeping record of 119 caps by Pat Jennings
of Northern Ireland. Without the competition from Shilton, Clemence was
capable of winning 130 caps for England. As it was, when Gordon Banks
retired in 1972, Shilton and Clemence spent the next two or three years
jockeying for position. Shilton was initially first choice, but Clemence
dominated the goalkeeping jersey between 1974 and 1978.

Ray was a different type of goalkeeper to Peter. He was a good shot-
stopper, but, at his peak, I think he was better than Peter at catching high
centres. He had very secure hands and seemed able to spring several feet
into the air, which was just as well because he wasn't particularly tall for a
goalkeeper. He had a lightweight build and was probably more athletic

Tom Finney   All-Sport

ABOVE: *Pat Jennings*
All-Sport/David Cannon

FAR LEFT: *Graeme Souness*
All-Sport/David Cannon

LEFT: *Jimmy Johnstone*
All-Sport/Don Morley

Bryan Robson   Colorsport

FAR LEFT: *Colin Bell*
Colorsport

LEFT: *Danny*
McGrain (*right*)
All-Sport/David Cannon

RIGHT: *Peter Shilton*
Bob Thomas

BELOW: *Kevin Keegan*
Colorsport

than Peter. I also think he was a great reader of the game and one of the first goalkeepers to act almost as a sweeper behind his back four. He had started his career with Scunthorpe, but when he joined Liverpool he found they played very square at the back. So Ray patrolled the edge of his area and was able to read situations very quickly, dashing from the box to boot away through balls. I think a lot of goalkeepers learned from him and that ploy is now standard practice.

Consistency was Ray's hallmark. He hardly missed a match during a wonderful career with Liverpool and probably picked up more honours at club level than any other goalkeeper.I think he had just one season when his standards dropped a little and that was in 1981–82 after Liverpool had sold him to Spurs. It was a decision that Liverpool may later have regretted.

Ray was 33 when he went to Spurs and I think the move jolted him a little because his first season at White Hart Lane was memorable largely for his hesitancy and lack of confidence. He hit one of those spells, rare in his career, when he was picking the ball out of the net on a regular basis. But he worked his way through the bad patch, buckled down in training – he was never as obsessive about training as Shilton – and soon recaptured his best form. Soon after moving to Spurs he announced his retirement from international football. He played the last of his 61 England games in Luxembourg in 1983 and I often wonder whether he felt he should have reconsidered his decision to quit the international arena.

I think Ray would have been recalled to the England squad had it not been for one or two newspaper articles in which he had been critical of manager Bobby Robson. The previous England manager, Ron Greenwood, had always said that he didn't have a number one goalkeeper. In his eyes Shilton and Clemence shared the honour equally – until it came to the 1982 World Cup in Spain and Greenwood chose Shilton. Ray had to sit on the substitute's bench for all five of England's World Cup games that summer; I felt it was a shame that Ray didn't get to play in the World Cup finals.

By 1987–88, after helping Spurs to reach the FA Cup final, injuries were affecting Ray's ability to maintain his previously high level of performance. With new manager Terry Venables rebuilding his squad, Ray was considering retirement. He played just 13 matches at the start of 1987–88, taking his career total to an incredible 1,119 first-team games. When Venables signed Bobby Mimms from Everton and Ray began helping with the coaching at White Hart Lane, it was clear that his playing days were over. So, at the age of 39, after a 23-season career that had earned him five First Division title medals, five FA Cup final appearances, three European Cup-winners' medals and an MBE in the Queen's Birthday Honours, Ray finally bowed out of the game he had graced for so long.

CHARLIE COOKE

Charlie Cooke (midfield)
Fife 14.10.42
Dundee United, Chelsea,
Crystal Palace
Scotland – 16

Charlie was one of those dazzling Scottish ball-playing wingers. He joined Chelsea from Dundee in 1966 and immediately became a great favourite at Stamford Bridge. He was a wonderful entertainer and possessed football's equivalent of the Ali shuffle – he had the ability to drop his shoulder, switch his point of balance and leave his marker stumbling about. It was a trick that usually brought the crowd out of their seats. He was a great dribbler and that was the essence of his game. I always thought him a good, accurate passer, too, but his ability to run with the ball and open up defences was the quality that earned him 16 Scottish caps.

Charlie played on the wing and in midfield and I think he was at his best playing in the thick of the action in the centre of the field where his close control was most valuable. He had a lot of Brazilian-style tricks – rolling the ball under his boot and dragging it away from defenders – and he was criticised for trying to beat the same defender three times just for the joy of it. People sometimes ask me if such trickery still has a place in the modern game. My answer is that it is the job of attacking players to open up opposing defences. Sometimes the simple pass does the job, other times the long through ball does it, but occasionally the pass is not the solution and you have to look for an alternative. Charlie Cooke and players like him provide that alternative. If he could get past one defender he would commit another defender to come away from the player he was marking and immediately a goalscoring opportunity would have been created.

Unfortunately this type of player is a dying breed; Charlie's elaborate dribbling skills would frustrate a lot of modern coaches who prefer to see everything methodical and rehearsed. Dave Sexton, the Chelsea manager during Cooke's best years, had to send him out on a Saturday afternoon knowing that he would do his own thing. He was an unpredictable player and there were obviously times when he should have released the ball earlier, but there were always occasions over 90 minutes when Charlie had the crowd purring with delight. You couldn't give Charlie a specific role and tell him: 'This is what I want you to do'. His skill was flamboyant and unconventional. He was the type of player around whom you had to build a system, giving him the freedom to use his talent as he thought best. Many of today's coaches would have a seizure if one of their players performed Cooke's trickery in their own half of the field.

He played 400 games for Chelsea in an 11-year spell that was interrupted by just one season when he was playing for Crystal Palace. He was a member of Tommy Docherty's bright young team which lost to Spurs in the 1967 FA Cup final and three years later he was back at Wembley, playing in the side that eventually beat Leeds in the FA Cup final replay. A year later he was a member of the Chelsea side that beat the mighty Real Madrid after a replay in the European Cup-winners' Cup final in Athens. Charlie often excelled against the lunging tackles of continental

OPPOSITE One of a dying breed: at the peak of his career Charlie Cooke brought crowds to their feet with his dribbling skills.

defenders, his balance neatly carrying him out of trouble. He was one of the great entertainers of his day and it is a shame that there appears to be no room for his type of player in the modern game.

TERRY COOPER

Terry Cooper (full back)
Castleford 12.7.44
Leeds United, Middlesbrough,
Bristol City, Bristol Rovers,
Doncaster Rovers
England – 20

At his peak Terry was probably the finest left back in the world. He started his career as a jinking winger and when 4–4–2 became fashionable after the 1966 World Cup he was successfully converted into a left back.

He came from the rugby league town of Castleford but his talent for soccer was quickly spotted by the Leeds United scouting system and he went to Elland Road in 1962. He was fortunate enough to be involved in the development of one of the most successful club sides of the last quarter of a century and became one of the key figures in the great Leeds side of the Don Revie era. He spent 12 seasons at Elland Road, forming a deadly attacking partnership on the left flank with Eddie Gray. I always reckoned that between them they provided a high percentage of Leeds United's goalscoring opportunities. The pinnacle of his career probably came in 1970 when he played in the Leeds side that finished second in the League championship, and lost the FA Cup final to Chelsea. At the end of the season he was in the England side that went to Mexico to defend the World Cup.

I thought he was a wonderful attacking defender but I think there was always a question mark about his defensive attributes. Like so many defenders who have strong attacking instincts, he was happiest when surging forward with the ball. This inevitably leaves gaps in the defence. I remember Jairzinho of Brazil turning Terry inside out in the heat of Mexico during the 1970 World Cup. I also remember Terry making some telling runs on the left flank. There's no doubt that he was a very exciting player at that time and was widely acknowledged as the best left back in the world, although I felt that West Germany's Paul Breitner was a more complete player in that position. Terry was a dogged competitior and, as was typical of most of that Leeds side, he didn't like to lose.

Terry had a slightly stooped stature which meant that he almost cast a shadow over the ball when he had it at his feet and was running at speed. He was difficult to knock off the ball and his excellent control and dribbling skills meant that he was always a threat to opposing teams on the left flank. He played 300 games for Leeds and won 20 England caps before moving to Middlesbrough in 1975. He spent three years at Ayresome Park, later playing for Bristol City, Bristol Rovers and Doncaster before going into management, with Bristol City in May 1982. In his six years of management at Ashton Gate he led the club out of Division Four and took them to two Freight Rover Trophy finals at Wembley. He also had the personal satisfaction of watching his son Mark, who had almost died of the bone disease osteomyelitis at the age of 15, develop as a young player on the City staff. In March 1988 City decided to dispense with Terry's managerial services but he bounced back two months later when, at the age of 44, he took on a fresh challenge as manager of Exeter City in the Fourth Division.

OPPOSITE *Terry Cooper of Leeds United, one of the best attacking full backs in the world in his time.*

STEVE COPPELL

Steve Coppell (winger)
Liverpool 9.7.55
Tranmere Rovers, Manchester
United
England – 42

Steve's career was unorthodox in that it didn't follow the normal pattern – from schoolboy forms, through the apprentice ranks to full professional. A thoughtful, scholarly lad who could often be found buried in some heavy reading material, he was considered too small to make the grade and he was a winger at a time when wingers were out of fashion. Nonetheless, when he was studying economics at Liverpool University, Tranmere rated

him highly enough to play him as an amateur in their Third Division side. Finally, he was forced to quit the game at the age of 28; it was a sad end to a career that was all too brief. Steve had enjoyed just 10 years at the top but in that time had made quite an impression. Tommy Docherty spotted his potential and signed him from Tranmere in 1975 when wingers were just coming back into fashion. He became one of the new breed of wide midfield players.

Sir Alf Ramsey's success with a 4–4–2 formation in 1966 had almost overnight halted the development of wingers but by the early 1970s managers and coaches were looking again for wide players who could both attack and defend and Steve was ideal for this job. He could wriggle past defenders, race to the line and send over a perfect cross, but he could also chase back and provide cover for the defenders on the right flank. He had a knack of cutting in from the right and hitting a crisp, waist high drive. He scored seven goals in 42 matches for England, and his biggest asset to the England team was his appetite for the ball and his willingness to tuck in and work back. When England lost possession Steve didn't stand out wide waiting for us to win back the ball. He wanted to win it back himself and he was involved all the time.

Steve came into the England side against Italy in 1977, making his debut with Manchester City's Peter Barnes, who played on the left flank. Bob Latchford and Kevin Keegan played in the middle and for quite a time that set-up looked like a very promising attack formation. Before each game the manager, Ron Greenwood, would insist to both wingers that they had to do their share of work in midfield. At that time Ray Wilkins and I were playing in the centre of midfield and not even our most avid admirers would claim that we were good tacklers. Subsequently, if we lost the ball we could be terribly exposed – which is precisely what happened in England's 4–3 defeat against Austria in Vienna in 1979. I must say, though, that Steve did his share of work that day, scoring one of the England goals. You could never point your finger at him and accuse him of hiding. As a midfield player I was often grateful for his presence. If nothing was going on down the middle of the pitch, I'd swing the ball out to the right because I knew that Steve would always be looking for it.

It was a great shame that his career was brought to an early end by a tackle from a Hungarian called Josef Toth at Wembley in November 1981. Steve struggled on for another 14 months but the condition of his knee deteriorated slowly, despite three operations. He was able to play in the first four games of the 1982 World Cup finals but the problem flared up again after the goalless draw against West Germany and he had to miss the next match against Spain. He was an essential element in the side and we never adequately compensated for his absence.

Steve played only two more games for England before finally hanging up his boots. He went into management with Crystal Palace and has shown the same dedication and enthusiasm there as he did as a player and chairman of the Professional Footballers' Association.

OPPOSITE *I often had cause to be grateful for Steve Coppell's presence in the England side. After his enforced retirement in 1984 it took England some time to fill the gap.*

RAY CRAWFORD

Ray Crawford (striker)
Portsmouth 13.7.36
Portsmouth, Ipswich Town,
Wolverhampton Wanderers,
West Bromwich Albion,
Charlton Athletic, Colchester
United
England – 2

I can recall sitting in the dressing room one Saturday afternoon in 1971 listening intently to the FA Cup results. Each result passed without causing any particular comment until we heard 'Colchester 3 Leeds United 2'. Little Colchester's triumph over mighty Leeds was one of the most amazing feats of giant killing in the history of the FA Cup. This was the Leeds of Bremner, Giles and Hunter, and Colchester was an indifferent Fourth Division side made up of untried youngsters, rejects from other clubs and ageing professionals coming towards the end of their careers. Into the last category came Ray Crawford, who was 35 when he helped to oust Don Revie's famous team from the FA Cup. In the 1950s and 1960s he had been a prolific goalscorer with six different clubs but I doubt if any moment in a distinguished career provided quite the same level of enjoyment as that afternoon against Leeds.

Probably the most sustained period of success in his career came in 1962 when he was the centre forward in Alf Ramsey's championship winning Ipswich team. Three players from that side have always stuck in my mind – a spindly little left winger called Jimmy Leadbetter, an inside forward who played alongside Ray, Ted Phillips, and Ray himself. I enjoyed watching all three play but I always considered Ray to be the star of the team.

He started his career with his local club, Portsmouth, and, after just one season, when he scored nine goals in 18 matches, they allowed him to go to Portman Road and it was at Ipswich that he really emerged as one of the outstanding goalscorers of his generation. He joined Ipswich in 1958 and in five seasons scored an incredible 142 goals in 197 games. His goalscoring consistency played a key role in helping Ipswich to win the Second and First Division titles in successive seasons and, not surprisingly, he was called into the England side in the championship year of 1962. He played only twice – making his debut against Northern Ireland and then scoring in a 3–1 win over Austria. In a sense he was unfortunate to be around at the same time as other accomplished England strikers like Jimmy Greaves. Crawford was an old fashioned type of centre forward and it was difficult for him to dislodge the players ahead of him in the England pecking order. At that time there was a surplus of players of similar style available to England, most notably Bobby Smith, with the glamorous Spurs side, and Gerry Hitchens, of Aston Villa and later Inter Milan.

Ray was an exuberant striker who could turn half chances into goals and he had all the basic assets of the classic centre forward – strength, courage and power in the air. He jumped well but, in my opinion, it was the timing of his runs that was his forte. He knew when to meet the ball, which is a great asset in a striker. I think he was probably slightly more mobile than many of the other central strikers of that time and it was his speed and endurance that allowed him to exploit defensive slackness. His goals quite rightly earned him a reputation as one of the most lethal marksmen of that era.

At the beginning of season 1963–64 Ray moved to Wolves and in 57 games for them he scored 39 goals which is a quite remarkable ratio by any standards. He then had one season at WBA before returning to Ipswich in March 1966. In three years he scored a further 61 goals in 123 games. His 203 goals in two spells at Ipswich still stands as the club record at Portman Road. In March 1969 he moved to Charlton and after just one season went to Colchester where he was to end his career in some style. Apart from helping to slay the mighty Leeds in the fifth round of the FA Cup he scored 25 goals in 45 matches that season, maintaining to the very end an insatiable appetite for goals.

Exuberant striker Ray Crawford was the cutting edge of the Ipswich team that took the First Division title in 1962 under Sir Alf Ramsey.

TONY CURRIE

Tony Currie (midfield)
Edgware 1.1.50
Watford, Sheffield United,
Leeds United, Queen's Park
Rangers, Torquay United
England – 17

Tony Currie battles for Sheffield
United against Spurs in 1972. A
flamboyant personality on and off
the field, he was a gifted long
passer.

Tony was an entertainer, the type of player that I miss in the game today. I suppose you have to bracket Tony alongside some of the other popular rebels I so liked to watch. He was a typical showman with a brashness bordering on arrogance, but he knew how to play the game. He was a fair-haired, scheming midfield player who appeared in Chelsea's junior side before joining Watford, although it was at Sheffield United that he really came to prominence and began to emerge as a player of immense talent. But, like so many players, he failed to totally fulfil his potential. He was a good all-rounder, primarily right footed, who could hit 50 to 60 yard passes that would land on a sixpence. He could also dribble with the ball and had a stunning long range shot that produced some spectacular goals, most notably at Sheffield United where he scored 55 in 300 games.

His long passing enabled him to switch the direction of attack superbly but he was sometimes criticised for not working hard enough and for not

taking enough defensive responsibility. I think at times that his fitness might have been a problem and that he might also have lacked a little dedication, which would explain his patches of inconsistent form. But when he was on song he was a player of immense talent and influence with Sheffield United, Leeds, QPR and England. He played 17 times for England, but should have played a lot more.

In 1973 when Sir Alf Ramsey was coming towards the end of his reign as manager, England played Austria at Wembley, winning 7–0 with Tony scoring one of the goals. Because the side had played so well, Alf kept the same 11 for a crucial World Cup qualifying tie against Poland at Wembley the following month. At that time it looked as though Tony was heading for a regular place in the England side but, largely because of the acrobatics of the Poland goalkeeper, Jan Tomaszewski, England could only draw 1–1 and thus failed to qualify for the World Cup. A few months later Alf was sacked and Tony's international career ground to an abrupt halt. He played only once in the next four years and it wasn't until 1978 that Ron Greenwood reinstated him in the squad on a regular basis.

In 1979 he joined QPR where his superb ball control and creative play on the artifical surface at Loftus Road helped them to reach the 1982 FA Cup final. Although Spurs won 1–0 in a replay I thought Currie made an outstanding contribution over the two games, but that was really the end of his career. Tony had a knee problem which, I suspect, wasn't helped by the artificial surface, and he later drifted around the backwaters of the game in Toronto, Chesham, Southend and Torquay.

KENNY DALGLISH

Kenny Dalglish MBE (striker)
Glasgow 4.3.51
Celtic, Liverpool
Scotland – 102

Kenny features very high in my top 100. From his earliest days at Celtic and throughout a marvellous career with Liverpool he has remained one of my favourite players. I remember him initially as a promising midfield player with Celtic who were rebuilding their team after winning the European Cup in 1967. He made his debut in 1970, gradually developing a sharp attacking instinct until he reached the point where he was the most prolific goalscorer in Scottish football. He scored at the rate of a goal a game in 200 matches over a six season spell.

When Liverpool sold Kevin Keegan to Hamburg in the summer of 1977 many felt that their domination of the English game would fade with the departure of such an influential player. How do you replace the irreplaceable? Liverpool decided that Dalglish was their man; he was signed from Celtic that summer and was an immediate success. The big red machine just kept rolling along.

Kenny became the key player in the Liverpool attack, his great strength being his ability to collect the ball with his back to the goal in the opposing penalty area. The way he twisted out of trouble, wrong footed defenders and hit short passes to create openings for others became the Dalglish trademark. Kenny was a player of tremendous talent, vision and awareness who could hit the telling pass that split a defence. Towards the end of his playing career he utilised this tactic more and more when he moved back into midfield.

He scored some spectacular goals and I particularly remember the one he scored in West Ham's Milk Cup final replay against Liverpool at Villa Park in 1981. West Ham were leading 1–0 when Terry McDermott chipped a ball through just to the right of our goal. Kenny was in the penalty area and as the ball floated over his shoulder he slid and hooked it in one movement right across the face of the goal into the far corner of the net. It was a quite remarkable goal and it laid the foundation for Liverpool's 2–1 victory. A youngster called Ian Rush, who had only just been signed from Chester, played in that replay. He is now, of course, a world class striker and I think Kenny played an influential role in his development. I'm sure Ian would be the first to admit that he has benefited enormously from the service Kenny provided in his days at Liverpool.

In the summer of 1985 Joe Fagan stepped down as manager following the Heysel Stadium disaster in the European Cup final in Brussels and Kenny was elevated to player–manager. Liverpool's success continued and Kenny, by this time 34, still made a contribution as a player. I felt he would have played more games had it not been for the problems involved in combining the two jobs. It was significant that in the 1985–86 season Dalglish played in only a handful of games in the first three-quarters of the season. In the final 12 games of which they won 11 and drew one, Dalglish played nine times scoring the only goal in the final match at Chelsea. It was the goal they needed to clinch the First Division title. When it mattered Dalglish rarely let Liverpool down.

A superb all-round creator and finisher, his only weakness was probably a lack of genuine pace. He won 102 caps for Scotland, a record, but never quite repeated his club form at international level. His trophies include three European Cup-winners' medals and seven League championship medals. Liverpool's 1986 First Division triumph coincided with an FA Cup final win over Everton at Wembley – giving Dalglish the coveted double in his first season in charge. A remarkable record for a remarkable player.

Liverpool's Kenny Dalglish hoists the FA Cup in 1986. His talents as a player and as a manager have earned him a prodigious collection of medals.

RON DAVIES

Ron Davies (striker)
Holywell 25.5.42
Chester City, Luton Town,
Norwich City, Southampton,
Portsmouth, Manchester
United, Millwall
Wales – 29

An old-fashioned centre forward,
Ron Davies had a good touch, but
he built his international
reputation on his heading ability.

Ron Davies was one of the most consistent post-war goalscorers and there was a time when his heading ability made him probably the most sought-after player in the First Division. Many people will remember him as one half of the great Wales twin spearhead of Ron Davies and Wyn Davies. They were equally effective in the air but I've chosen Ron to join my 100 greatest because I feel he had a better touch on the ground and greater awareness of the game than Wyn. Ron probably lacked some of Wyn's tenacity, but he compensated for that with the quality of his all-round game, his composure in front of the goal and his superiority in the air. He was more than 6 ft tall which gave him an obvious advantage in airborne duels but his secret was not his ability to jump high but his ability to remain in the air for longer than anyone else, which is something few strikers can do well. Joe Royle could do it and so could a former team-mate of mine at West Ham, Billy Jennings. They spring that little bit earlier than most defenders, often with their elbows splayed out like wings, so the marking

defender, who jumps fractionally later, can't get above them to challenge for the ball.

Ron was born in Holywell and began his professional career with Chester in 1959, where he spent three years scoring 44 goals in 94 matches and quickly establishing a reputation as a goalscorer. Luton Town signed him for £10,000 in 1962 and after scoring 21 goals for them in just 32 matches he moved to Norwich. It was while at Carrow Road that he won the first of his 29 Wales caps. He scored in his debut game against Northern Ireland and, having established his goalscoring pedigree, went on to partner Wyn Davies in a spectacular attacking spearhead.

His £55,000 transfer from Norwich to Southampton in 1966 elevated him to superstar status. Almost overnight he became one of the most talked-about strikers in the First Division. He was getting his blond head to centres from Terry Paine and John Sydenham so regularly that, at some stage or other during his seven years at the Dell, transfer speculation linked his name with all the major clubs in the First Division. He remained loyal to Southampton, though, and must have had a great influence on the development of Mike Channon. When Ron first joined Southampton he partnered Martin Chivers in attack for a while, but the greater part of his time with the club was spent alongside the young Channon, who of course went on to play for England.

After scoring 134 goals in around 250 matches, Ron moved along the south coast to Portsmouth where he spent just one season. In 1974, at the age of 32, he joined Tommy Docherty's Manchester United, but by then Ron's great days were over and he couldn't establish himself in the first team. He finished his career the following season with a few games at Millwall. At his peak he was one of the game's most feared strikers and, throughout a 16-year career he scored at the rate of a goal every other game. He had a younger brother, Paul, who played for Arsenal and Charlton, but who was never able to match the achievements of Ron.

ALAN DEVONSHIRE

Alan Devonshire (winger)
Park Royal 13.4.56
West Ham United
England – 8

During my career at West Ham there were three team-mates I particularly enjoyed playing alongside. The first was Billy Bonds, who acted as my 'minder' over the years, the second was Bryan 'Pop' Robson, who was a great finisher and wonderful target man for me, and the third was Alan Devonshire. Over an eight-year period 'Dev' and I developed a sound understanding at West Ham and I have always thought it a shame that we never got the chance to explore fully the partnership on an international stage.

Dev was a late developer in the professional game and must be an inspiration to all those youngsters who are passed over by the big clubs in their teens and who fear that they have lost their only opportunity. I also sensed with him that he was a little more appreciative of his career than many other professionals largely because he had spent the first years of his working life in a factory. When you have tasted the alternatives, professional football doesn't seem such a bad way to earn a living. His father, Les, had been an outside left with Brentford (playing in the same side as Ron Greenwood), Chester and Crystal Palace, though young Alan didn't get his chance in the professional game until he was 20. He was working in the Hoover factory in west London and playing for Southall in the old Isthmian League when Ron, then the West Ham manager, signed him for £5,000.

I remember Alan walking through the door for the first time at our training ground at Chadwell Heath; there was nothing of him and I just couldn't imagine him coming to terms with the physical demands of the First Division. But he was soon in the side, making his debut in a League Cup tie against Queen's Park Rangers in October 1976. We were beaten 2–0 but Dev played well and kept his place in the team for the rest of the season. Initially, he played on the right but, although he was naturally right footed, he really made his name with those long, elusive runs when he switched to the left flank. In those days his greatest strength was his speed; he possessed an extra gear that enabled him to step up his pace to outstrip an opponent. He had such acceleration that you knew that if you played the ball into space he would almost certainly get past defenders and reach it first.

For such a lightweight player – he always looks to me as though he could do with a good meal – he possesses prodigious stamina and towards the end of my playing career I suppose it's fair to say that he became my 'legs'. His fine balance enables him to ride the most robust of tackles and there is no doubt in my mind that, at his peak, he was one of the most exciting players in the game. He made his England debut during Greenwood's reign as manager in 1980. At that time Ron was playing with two wingers and I often felt that Alan would have been the ideal player to have on the left flank, but he played only eight times and was never able to establish himself. This was a pity because, as I said, I would have liked

the opportunity to see if we could have repeated our club performances together at international level. As it was, I played alongside him only once in an England shirt — on his debut against Northern Ireland.

I feel England never saw the best of Alan. His game was built on short passing; he would pick up the ball, beat a defender, run with it, hit a short pass and then move into space to receive the return. He had a good understanding with Paul Goddard and myself at West Ham, but there was no one in the England side who would move into space to collect Dev's passes and utilise his strengths. Peter Beardsley, as he plays now, would probably have been a good foil for Dev. Sadly, those days of the long surging runs and international recognition are over because of a terrible injury he sustained in January 1984. West Ham were in the top three in the League title race when we met Wigan in the third round of the FA Cup at Upton Park. Dev, as he did so often, toe-ended the ball into space and was chasing after it when he was caught simultaneously by two challenges coming from opposite directions. At first, we thought it was a minor injury but, in fact, he had snapped the ligaments in a knee. It was 19 months before he was back in the first team on a regular basis.

With Alan out of the side West Ham's chances of winning the title in 1984 faded considerably. I had pencilled in that summer to retire and when I realised that he wasn't going to be fit to play the following season I went ahead and hung up my boots. Dev's injury was a big influence on my decision; had he been fit I would probably have played for another season because I felt that with him in the side that West Ham team had a realistic chance of winning the First Division championship. Significantly, when he finally regained his fitness, he helped West Ham to finish third in 1985–86 — their highest ever League placing. Although still a key player, the greyhound speed had gone so he had to adjust his game and adopt a more thoughtful style. It's a great credit to his resilient nature that he has been able to resurrect a career that could easily have been ended by such a horrific injury.

If he has a flaw in his game it is that he can't shoot, not even after all these years of practice. Considering the amount of possession he has had over the years, and the speed with which he has cut into shooting positions from midfield, he has been a poor goalscorer — probably worse than me, which shows how bad he is! One Devonshire goal I do remember, though, came in the FA Cup semi-final replay against Everton at Elland Road in 1980. Dev ran his marking full back, John Gidman, ragged that night and scored West Ham's first goal in a 2–1 win. That was probably the finest match Dev ever played for West Ham.

DEREK DOUGAN

To describe Derek Dougan as a colourful character would be something of an understatement; he was an extrovert who became a marvellous centre forward. I can remember him sporting a skinhead-type haircut, then a Mohican haircut and, when he got bored with that, he had long, straggly hair and a Mexican bandit-type moustache. He was the sort of player who drew the crowds through the turnstiles and, if at times he went a little over the top, I still feel that it's a shame that his kind of personality is disappearing from the game.

He was born in Belfast and played for Distillery before joining Portsmouth in 1957. The following year he made his debut for Northern Ireland against Czechoslovakia, playing in the same side as Danny Blanchflower and Harry Gregg, but he struggled initially to establish himself in the Football League. He went to Blackburn Rovers and Aston Villa and drifted into the Third Division with Peterborough where his 38 goals in 77 matches convinced the bigger clubs that he still had a lot to offer. In May 1965 Leicester City signed him and he scored 35 goals for them in two years, but it wasn't until he joined Wolves in March 1967, helping them to clinch promotion from Division Two, that he began to emerge as more than just a colourful character.

Derek Dougan (striker)
Belfast 20.1.38
Distillery, Portsmouth,
Blackburn Rovers, Aston Villa,
Peterborough United, Leicester
City, Wolverhampton
Wanderers
Northern Ireland — 43

Derek 'the Doog' Dougan scored 93 goals in 250 games at Wolves, proving that he was more than just a colourful character.

Already a great favourite with the fans, Derek became one of the most explosive and exciting strikers in the First Division. In eight years at Wolves he scored 93 goals in 250 games. He helped them to reach the UEFA Cup final, where they lost to Spurs in 1972, and he played in the side that beat Manchester City 2–1 in the 1974 League Cup final. Alongside him in that very good Wolves team were players like Mike Bailey, Ken Hibbitt, John Richards, Peter Knowles and David Wagstaffe. There were times when Derek – 'The Doog' to his team-mates – must have been particularly grateful for the service he received from Wagstaffe, a very quick and direct left winger who supplied a stream of passes to central strikers.

Dougan was tall, lean, awkward and had thin sharp features that always reminded me of the American film actor Lee Van Cleef. Derek used to run and jump for high balls with his elbows jutting out and there is no doubt that he was a prickly kind of striker who used to niggle opposing defenders. After marking him for 90 minutes, most centre halves would come off the field knowing they had been in a tough match.

He was the tenacious, old fashioned type of centre forward who battled for everything – and usually won. He did exceptionally well in the air but it's not so readily acknowledged that he was also skilled on the ground. I thought he had outstanding ball control with his left foot and was particularly good at holding up play while waiting for team-mates to join him. With his back to the goal, he could pass to either flank, drawing team-mates into the attacking situation, spin away from his marker and, with long legs pumping and elbows flying, he would race towards the goal for the return ball.

He would frequently wave his arms to team-mates to demand the ball when he was in full stride. He was a very volatile character whose thoughts about the game could be outrageous and he didn't go out of his way to endear himself to referees or the game's authorities although he later became a respected chairman of the Professional Footballers' Association.

Derek retired in 1974 after a 17-year career during which he became one of Northern Ireland's most capped strikers. Regularly playing alongside Pat Jennings, Terry Neill and George Best in one of Northern Ireland's finest teams, he won a total of 43 caps which must have compensated in part for missing out on the domestic game's major honours.

BRYAN DOUGLAS

Bryan Douglas was a brilliant, ball-playing forward who made up for a lack of height and physical strength – he was only 5 ft 6 in – with great vision and artistry. He spent his entire career with Blackburn Rovers and played 36 times for England. He was born in Blackburn and joined his home town team as a groundstaff boy in 1952. Two years later he made his first team debut. He was basically an orthodox right winger, the position he played when he wore an England shirt, but he eventually settled down with Rovers as an inside right.

I remember watching him in that very good Blackburn side of the 1960s when he, and players like Ron Clayton and Fred Pickering, made them one of the finest teams in the First Division. He hit his passes beautifully and used to sit in the centre of midfield knocking the ball around. Essentially a short passer, he had the knack of clipping balls forward to his front strikers. I think it's fair to say that he wasn't a lover of the physical side of the game and I suspect that he would have been intimidated by some of the tackling and marking we see today. I always enjoyed watching him and particularly remember his virtuoso performance when Blackburn beat West Ham 8–2 at Upton Park in 1963–64.

That result remains West Ham's record home defeat and, although Fred Pickering and Peter McEvoy each scored a hat trick, there was no doubt that Bryan was the executioner-in-chief. Blackburn were the League leaders at the time, unbeaten in their previous 10 matches, and West Ham simply could not control Bryan's creative flair in the midfield area. Even on a muddy pitch the little fellow was the most influential figure on the field.

His performance that day probably cost Martin Peters his place in the West Ham side that played Preston in the FA Cup final a few months later. That defeat came on Boxing Day 1963 and, because of the way the fixtures were arranged at that time, West Ham travelled to Blackburn to meet Rovers again two days later. For this game the manager, Ron Greenwood, dropped Martin and brought in Eddie Bovington, basically a defensive midfield player whom Ron hoped could do a good marking job on Bryan. The outcome of that tactical switch was that West Ham won 3–1 – Johnny Byrne scoring two goals and Geoff Hurst the third. Thereafter, Martin was out, and stayed out, and when West Ham met Preston at Wembley Eddie was still in the team. This was just one of many occasions on which managers were forced to make tactical changes to cater for the talent of Bryan Douglas.

He had helped Rovers to win promotion from Division Two in 1957–58 when they finished one point behind West Ham. That was the season he made his England debut against Wales wearing Stanley Matthews' number seven shirt. Considering that Bryan played in the era of Matthews, Finney, Greaves, Charlton and Haynes he did well to get 36 caps. The England coach Don Howe, who played in the same side as Bryan, compared

Bryan Douglas (midfield)
Blackburn 27.5.34
Blackburn Rovers
England – 36

England's thrusting young winger, Bryan Douglas, signs autographs before the 1958 World Cup. He later switched very successfully to a midfield role.

him to a counter-punching boxer. 'He used to tempt the defender to lunge in and just as he made his move, he would jink away out of trouble and fly down the right flank', recalls Howe. 'He was a lovely crosser of the ball'.

Douglas could also score goals – 13 in 36 games for England, which is an excellent return for a winger. He also scored more than 100 goals for Rovers in 438 League matches between 1954–68. Probably the two high points in Bryan's distinguished career were playing in the 1960 FA Cup final, where Rovers lost 3–0 to Wolves, and then playing in all four of England's games in the 1962 World Cup in Chile. He left Blackburn in 1968 and spent a couple of seasons playing non-League football for Great Harwood before retiring from the game.

GEORGE EASTHAM

George Eastham was not only a remarkable player, but a remarkable man, too. He had the courage to take on the football establishment and was largely responsible for the removal of the maximum wage in 1961. He brought the whole question of players' conditions and contracts into the open and into the courts when Newcastle refused to give him a transfer. Victory for Eastham, and the Professional Footballers' Association, meant that men who had been restricted to a maximum £20 a week could command three or four times that amount. Within a year of Eastham's historic court action Fulham were paying their England captain, Johnny Haynes, £100 a week. Today's big-name players can earn £3,000 a week. All professional footballers should be grateful to George Eastham.

He was a man of great conviction with a pioneering spirit, but he was no blustering, tub-thumping politician as you might have expected of someone who fought for players' rights and brought about such sweeping changes in the game. Looking at George you would never have imagined him to be a professional footballer. There was nothing of him; he was one of the slimmest, frailest players I've ever seen but he had a wonderful, natural talent. He had superb balance and the ability to run and dribble with the ball almost as if it were tied to his feet. Nimble-footed, he was able to swivel and change direction with ease and, no matter how tight the marking, he could always make the space to pass to either flank.

George came from a footballing family in Blackpool; his father, also called George, played for Blackpool, Swansea, Rochdale and Lincoln, and his uncle Henry played for Liverpool, Tranmere and Accrington. They were a northern family and I suppose young George grew up to value northern, working class standards. He began his professional career with Newcastle in 1956 and, after playing around 150 games for them, he sought Queen's Counsel's opinion that players' contracts were unfairly restrictive, and finally won a determined fight to be allowed to join Arsenal in 1960. Arsenal paid a fee of £47,500; only Denis Law had cost more on the transfer market – when he moved from Huddersfield to Manchester City for £55,000.

In six years at Arsenal George scored 41 goals in 207 matches. He was a very neat, short-passing player – 10 or 15 yard passes were his speciality – and he always put exactly the right weight on the ball. One man who must have been immensely impressed by George's midfield contribution at Highbury was Alf Ramsey, who had recently been installed as England manager, because Eastham was one of his first selections. George made his debut against Brazil in 1963 and was a regular in the number 10 shirt until just before the 1966 World Cup. By this time he was 30, and had played a total of 19 games for England.

Soon after the World Cup final he moved to Stoke where, despite the onrushing years, he enjoyed probably the most fruitful period of his career. In those days he was the midfield 'brain' in a Stoke side that included Peter

George Eastham OBE
(midfield)
Blackpool 23.9.36
Ards, Newcastle United,
Arsenal, Stoke City
England – 19

Dobing, Jimmy Greenhoff, John Ritchie, Gordan Banks, Denis Smith and Micky Bernard, a young ball-winner there to 'protect' the older element in the team. It was a good side and I will never forget the gruelling series of matches that West Ham played against them in the old League Cup in 1972. George was approaching 36 yet he remained an inspirational figure in Stoke's midfield. We won the first leg of the semi-final 2–1 at Stoke but they then won 1–0 during a famous encounter at Upton Park, Banks' save from a Geoff Hurst penalty costing us a place at Wembley.

A third game at Hillsborough ended goalless so we went to Old Trafford for another replay. A crowd of 50,000 packed into the ground that night and they saw a spectacular match. We lost 3–2 in quite dramatic fashion when our goalkeeper, Bobby Ferguson, was injured and Bobby Moore had to go in goal. He saved a penalty but Peter Dobing hit in the rebound. I was bitterly disappointed at the time but, looking back, it was all exciting stuff. So, Stoke went to Wembley where they beat Chelsea 2–1 in the final and guess who scored the winning goal – George Eastham did. He played a few more games for Stoke, but that Wembley winner was really the last great moment in a long and distinguished career.

For a man of slight build, George Eastham had a wonderful touch and balance – essential for inside forwards in those days of heavy, laced footballs.

DUNCAN EDWARDS

No one can say how good a player Duncan Edwards might have become – they can only say how good he was. I once read Bobby Charlton describe him as 'the greatest of them all'. I never saw Duncan play but there is no doubt that in a professional career that lasted only five years he made a phenomenal impression on the game. He must have had a very special talent. He was in the Munich air disaster of 1958 and survived in hospital for 15 days after the crash. He was 21 when he died.

Duncan made his debut for Manchester United in 1953 at the age of 16 and at the age of 18 years and 183 days he became the youngest player to wear the white shirt of England in a full international, against Scotland in April 1955. It was a record that still stood 33 years later. Before he died he played 18 times for England, won two League championship medals and played in an FA Cup final for United. He captained England at schoolboy and Under–23 level and would surely have gone on to lead his country at the highest level of all.

There was, of course, an immense feeling of loss in the country when the Manchester United plane crashed on the way home from a European Cup tie in Belgrade. Matt Busby had built a wonderful team and Duncan was one of eight 'Busby Babes' to die in the crash. I wasn't a United fan, but they had players I admired, notably Duncan Edwards and Tommy Taylor. I was only 10 when the tragedy happened but old enough to realise that the English game had lost a great team and some talented individual players.

Don Howe, who was Ron Greenwood's coach during my England days, was a close friend of Duncan's and a bearer at his funeral. Don came from Sedgely, near Wolverhampton, and Duncan was from the next town, Dudley. 'Duncan was a colossus even as a boy', Don told me. 'He was essentially a left half, but could play just as comfortably at centre half or centre forward. They once played him up front in the England Under–23 team and he scored six goals. He was a good passer, powerful in the air and could hit shots from all over the place, and for such a powerful boy he had a very delicate touch.'

Don remembers him as a solid, square-built player, just under six feet tall with immensely powerful thighs. He tackled with the force of an earth moving machine and when he scored a 25-yard goal against the West Germans in 1955 – his shot deposited the goalkeeper in the back of the net – the German press nicknamed him 'Boom Boom'. Apart from his power, he had a splendid touch on the ball and was quick for a heavily built man. When he was 15 Matt Busby said of him, 'He looks and plays like a man'. Busby used to watch him play for United's junior squad to see if he could find some fault in his game but he never could.

I often wonder what sort of career he would have enjoyed had it not been for the Munich disaster and I can remember reading that Duncan

Duncan Edwards (centre back)
Dudley 1.10.36 died 21.2.58
Manchester United
England – 18

Duncan Edwards (centre) trains with England colleague Stanley Matthews (left) and captain Billy Wright. Many observers believed he could have become one of the greatest half backs in history.

Edwards was the player around whom the future England team would be built. Would Bobby Moore have had such a long and distinguished international career had Duncan lived? He would have been 30 at the time of the 1966 World Cup final and probably ideal captaincy material. The fact that people still talk about Duncan with such affection and, sometimes, in such awed tones, speaks volumes about the impression he made on the game in five short years.

MIKE ENGLAND

Mike was probably one of the best centre halves of the last 25 years and he had all the strengths I look for in a central defender. He was a superb player for Blackburn Rovers, Tottenham, Cardiff and Wales; he was multi-talented and, although a defender by choice, he played the occasional, brilliant game at centre forward.

Mike was born in Prestatyn and began his career with Blackburn in 1959. In six years he played nearly 200 games for them, winning the first of 44 Welsh caps against Northern Ireland in 1962 at the age of 21. He was a stubborn and fiercely ambitious player and when Rovers initially refused to allow him to try his luck with a bigger club he threatened to quit the game altogether. After a series of transfer requests Rovers finally relented and sold him to the mighty Tottenham Hotspur in 1966 for £95,000, which was a record sum for a defender at the time. Tottenham were still trying to complete their rebuilding programme after the break up of the 1961 double side and England's influence was immediate. They won the FA Cup in 1967 and, with England a 6 ft 2 in pillar of strength and durability in the heart of their defence, followed this with the League Cup in 1971, the UEFA Cup in 1972 and the League Cup again in 1973.

In my opinion he was one of Bill Nicholson's greatest captures. 'I signed him because he liked heading the ball', recalled the Spurs manager of the time, 'that's the major part of the job for a player in that position'. If that sounds like an over simplification, it was nonetheless the main reason for Nicholson's choice. He needed to fortify a team that was laden with wonderful attacking players like Jimmy Greaves and Alan Gilzean and formidable midfield players like Dave Mackay and Alan Mullery. Mike's authority and power in the air was probably his single greatest asset, not just defensively, but in attacking positions too.

When West Ham played Spurs in those days we were always concerned about Mike's presence at set-pieces. He would run in for headers at corner kicks and free kicks and his power and bravery made him an intimidating opponent to mark. Tottenham regularly used a tactic which involved Mike getting his head to a long throw-in from Martin Chivers. An expert with the long throw, Martin's job was to pick out England or Alan Gilzean, who were both brilliant in the air: England and Gilzean would take turns to stand closer to goal and Chivers would let them know which one was to receive the ball by holding it in a pre-arranged hand – the left hand for one player and the right for the other. It usually worked but there were occasions when Chivers forgot which hand to use and then the result was quite farcical!

I think Mike and Alan Mullery provided the heart and guts of the Spurs side during that period. They were quality performers striving to match the standards set in 1961 – a hard act to follow – but they were the sort of characters who thrived on just such challenges. Mike's other great quality

Mike England MBE (centre back)
Prestatyn 2.12.41
Blackburn Rovers, Tottenham Hotspur, Cardiff City
Wales – 44

was his patience. He was a taut, crisp tackler but, unlike a lot of defenders, he didn't dive into a challenge; he read the situation and would jockey opponents, waiting for the right moment before striking with precision.

I mentioned earlier that he was stubborn and, having played golf with him, I know how strong-minded he can be. Well, in February 1975, with Tottenham at this time fighting hard to avoid relegation, he suddenly announced that he had played his last game for the club. Terry Neill, then the manager at White Hart Lane, tried to persuade him to change his mind but Mike said that he was no longer enjoying the game and felt that his best days were over. What he failed to say was that he disagreed with the way the team and club were being run. His last game for Spurs was a 3–0 defeat at home to Leicester when he was 31. At the end of the season Spurs avoided relegation by just one point. I think Mike may have regretted leaving Spurs on such an impulse. The following season he played 40 games for Cardiff, helping them to win promotion from Division Three. He then spent a couple of years playing soccer in the United States before returning to Britain where he eventually became manager of the Welsh national side.

Positive and forthright as a player, he carried the same virtues into management. He proved to be a diligent manager and, although working with limited resources, he had the bonus of being able to call upon great players of the calibre of Ian Rush, Mark Hughes and Kevin Ratcliffe. But then Wales' failure to qualify for the European Championships prompted the Welsh FA to sack England in 1988.

Welshman Mike England was a key element in the rebuilding of the Tottenham side following the break-up of the legendary double team.

TOM FINNEY

At the peak of Tom Finney's career he was spoken of in the same breath as Sir Stanley Matthews – and there were many people in the game who thought him a better all-round player. He retired in 1959 at the age of 38, having devoted his entire career to Preston North End and England. I never saw him in action but I have childhood memories of watching him on television and, since then of course, I've watched clips of him many times.

One of the game's great debates over the years has revolved around Matthews and Finney, wing partners in more than 20 England teams. Who was the better player? Matthews had a presence that endeared him to millions and was a wonderfully gifted player but many of those who played with and against both of them reckon that Finney was the better of the two. I once remember reading the opinions of the legendary Bill Shankly, purring over the talent of Finney; the only criticism he could make of Finney was that he didn't play for Liverpool! He reckoned that Finney was the best attacking player he had ever seen. 'If I were pressed into it, I would say that Tommy was the best player ever born', wrote Shankly.

Finney was certainly the more versatile of the two men, able to play with equal ease on the right or left flank and, indeed, late in his career he proved to be an accomplished centre forward. He could create and score goals and had the little bit of magic that turned matches and rescued lost causes. He joined Preston in 1937 and turned professional in 1940 upon completing a plumbing apprenticeship and, from then on, he was known throughout his career as 'The Preston Plumber'. He scored 187 goals in 433 games for Preston and was one of the few players to be voted Footballer of the Year twice – in 1954 and 1958. Sadly, the major domestic honours eluded him. He played in the 1954 FA Cup final when Preston lost 3–2 to WBA and in 1957–58 – when he played at centre forward and scored 26 goals – he helped Preston to the runners-up spot behind Wolves in the First Division.

He played most of his games for Preston on the right wing, which was his favourite position, but almost half of his 76 England games were played on the left wing without the slightest detriment to his effectiveness. In fact, he scored 30 goals for England – only Bobby Charlton and Jimmy Greaves have scored more for England since the war. He made his England debut in 1947 and had a 12-year international career. Had he played nowadays when the international side averages about one game a month if they are successful in the big tournaments, he would have won well over 100 caps.

Ron Greenwood, my manager at both club and international level, played against both Matthews and Finney and, like Shankly, Ron is one of those people who considers Finney to be the more complete player. Ron first saw Finney play in the war-time Cup final against Arsenal when, as a youngster still to make his name, Tom turned the England captain, Eddie Hapgood, inside out. Ron considers Finney to be better than Matthews because 'he

Tom Finney OBE (winger)
Preston 5.4.22
Preston North End
England – 76

*The versatile Tom Finney –
Preston North End Footballer of
the Year, 1954. A uniquely
talented attacking player, he was
equally effective on either wing or
at centre forward.*

simply had more to offer'. Like Matthews, Finney made long, shimmying runs followed by precision crosses. He may not have had Matthews' craft with the ball at his feet but, for a man of 10 stone, he had enormous resilience, could shoot and head powerfully and had the cunning that turned a good pass into a brilliant one. Apart from driving a tank around Egypt for a few years during the war and tinkering with dripping taps, Tom's life revolved around Deepdale and Preston. He was born there and he retired there. He was a £20 a week man until the end of his career but there is no doubt that his reputation and status helped to create the climate for the removal of the maximum wage in 1961.

When I first went to West Ham, Bobby Moore used to tell the youngsters at the club about the great Tom Finney. They were from a different era, but Bobby played alongside Tom in 1960. It was Bobby's first trip with the Football Association and they had persuaded Tom Finney to come out of retirement to make a few guest appearances at various points around the globe. As it turned out he was the only player on the trip to appear in all 11 matches. According to Bobby it was an education to play in the same team with Tom. 'He had a lovely, natural ability and was equally adept with either foot', said Bobby. 'And he was a charming, modest man, too'. Shankly used to say that Finney would have been great in any team, in any age, in any match 'even if he had been wearing an overcoat'.

TREVOR FRANCIS

A footballing prodigy in his teens, Trevor never fulfilled the extravagant predictions that accompanied his arrival on the scene in 1970. He showed enormous potential when he broke into the Birmingham City side as a 16 year old. The headlines tagged him 'the wonder boy of the 1970s' but, for me, there was always a big question mark over his fitness. There is no doubt that he was quite outstanding as a youngster, initially scoring goals at the rate of one a game; for a while we really thought that a footballing genius had landed among us.

He ran well with the ball, had genuine pace, could go past defenders with ease and could score confidently with a shot or header. He seemed to be the perfect striker. He benefited hugely from playing alongside some talented and very experienced strikers like Bob Hatton and Bob Latchford and quickly became the favourite of the crowd at St Andrews. After eight

Trevor Francis (striker)
Plymouth 19.4.54
Birmingham City, Nottingham Forest, Manchester City, Sampdoria, Atalanta, Glasgow Rangers, Queen's Park Rangers
England – 52

England striker Trevor Francis under pressure from Finland's Leo Houtsonen (left) in 1985. Sadly, Francis's career was handicapped by a series of injuries.

years at Birmingham, scoring more than 100 goals in 300 games, he created a little bit of soccer history by becoming football's first £1 million player.

Brian Clough decided he was worth such a massive investment and signed him for Nottingham Forest in February 1979. Trevor wasn't renowned for his heading, but three months later he repaid a big slice of the fee when he headed the winning goal in the European Cup final against Malmö of Sweden in Munich. The following season he was again an influential figure in the Forest side that achieved success by winning the European Cup for a second time. By this time he was an established England player though a catalogue of injuries interrupted his career both at international and club level at regular intervals.

Trevor had made his England debut against Holland on a grim night at Wembley when the Dutch won 2–0 in February 1977. In all he made 52 England appearances, played in the 1982 World Cup in Spain and was slightly unfortunate, I thought, not to be in the squad for the 1986 World Cup in Mexico. The previous summer he had played against Italy and Mexico in a World Cup warm-up competition in Mexico City and had looked the best of the England strikers in both those games. He never really got a look in after that trip, playing just once more against Scotland, before the England squad departed for the World Cup.

He was a player of tremendous speed and I often wonder whether it was the fact that he took so many knocks and fell so heavily when in full stride that caused his frequent injuries. Whatever the reasons, I felt his best years were his early days with Birmingham. Forest recouped their £1 million by selling him to Manchester City, who then sold him to Sampdoria in Italy for £800,000 in July 1982.

He finished his playing career in Italy with Atalanta of Bergamo and then, somewhat surprisingly, Glasgow Rangers signed him at the beginning of the 1987–88 season. Rangers manager Graeme Souness had played with Francis in Italy and knew him well. That meant, of course, that Graeme knew of Trevor's bad luck with injuries so Rangers offered him a contract that was reputedly worth £1,000 a match ... but only for the matches he played.

Trevor spent just nine months with Rangers and once they had been knocked out of the European Cup in 1988 Souness decided to release him on a free transfer. So six years after joining the exodus to Italy, he returned to the English First Division with QPR at the age of 34. Of course, he was no longer the quicksilver striker who had scored a sensational 15 goals in 21 matches in his first season at Birmingham. But, if his pace had slackened, his touch was still good and his experience could prove invaluable. The Queen's Park Rangers' manager, Jim Smith – the man who had sold him from Birmingham to Forest for £1 million – reckoned Trevor could help his young team as they pushed for the runners-up position at the end of the 1987–88 League championship. Trevor leapt at the chance of returning to First Division football and signed a contract lasting until the end of the 1988–89 season.

ARCHIE GEMMILL

Archie Gemmill was an exuberant little midfield player whose persistence and relentless energy were wonderfully illustrated by the goal he scored for Scotland against Holland in the 1978 World Cup in Argentina. He had already scored from the penalty spot to give the Scots a 2–1 lead when he picked up the ball wide on the right in the sixty-eighth minute of a decisive qualifying match. Like an Alpine skier negotiating the slalom, Gemmill threaded his way through the Dutch defence, evading three challenges before hitting a raking shot from 25 yards past Jan Jongbloed. It was a superb solo goal and *El Grafico*, the Argentine sports magazine, claimed it to be the best of the tournament. Sadly, the Scots needed to win by three clear goals to qualify for the next stage of the tournament. They got the three goals – thanks largely to Gemmill – but the final result, 3–2, was enough to put the Dutch through on goal difference.

I would have liked to have seen Scotland progress for Gemmill's sake if for no other reason. He was one of the best left sided midfield players around during my career and I was always a little in awe of his energy – and envious, too! He was a busy, dynamic player who snapped away at the opposition like a Scottish terrier. He was only 5 ft 5 in, but he made up for a lack of height with tremendous enthusiasm and determination. Born in Paisley, he began his career with St Mirren in 1964 and played about 80 games for them before joining Preston North End for £16,000 in June 1967. After three years he moved to Derby County for £60,000 and it was under the management of Brian Clough that his career really began to take off. Clough loved him, and particularly the competitive edge he brought to every game. At this time Derby had one of the finest teams in Europe and the tough, ebullient Gemmill provided the hard core in midfield. He played a significant role in helping Derby to win the League title in 1972 and again in 1975.

What were his strengths? He had a good all-round game and, like a lot of the small midfield players I've selected, he had a burning desire to succeed and be a winner. A non-stop 90-minute competitor, he was at his best in the attacking sense when running with the ball. He wasn't a great passer, preferring to play the ball in to the front men and then run to accept the return pass. You rarely saw him hit long, telling passes as he was essentially a fetcher and carrier. This industrious side to his nature obviously appealed to Clough. After he quit as Derby County manager he had spells with Brighton and Leeds before moving to Nottingham Forest in January 1975. When he realised in season 1977–78 that he was close once again to a championship winning team he went back to Derby to sign Gemmill. Forest paid £100,000 plus goalkeeper John Middleton in September 1977.

Archie was so highly rated by the Derby fans that he was obliged by new manager Tommy Docherty to sign a written transfer request, thus forfeiting his share of the transfer fee. Docherty explained at the time, 'I

Archie Gemmill (midfield)
Paisley 24.3.47
St Mirren, Preston North End, Derby County, Nottingham Forest, Birmingham City, Wigan Athletic
Scotland – 43

think it's only fair that the club should not be blamed by the supporters for getting rid of him'. Well, Gemmill went straight into the Forest side and played 32 games, finishing on the losing side only twice. At the end of the season he picked up his third League championship medal. The following season he played a significant role in helping Forest to reach the European Cup final – but he didn't play on the big day. He was on the substitute's bench, his place taken by Ian Bowyer, when Forest beat Malmö of Sweden 1–0 in Munich in 1979.

By this time Gemmill was 32 and, if his athleticism was fading, he had lost none of his organisational ability. He was the sort of player who coaxed the best out of those around him and for that reason Birmingham signed him in August 1979 and he repaid them by helping to clinch promotion from Division Two in his first season at St Andrews. He was still a valued member of the Scotland squad and didn't play the last of his 43 games for his country until 1981. Soon after that he had a spell in America with Jacksonville, returning to England to play a handful of games for Wigan before ending his big-time career with his old club, Derby County.

A fiercely competitive Scottish terrier in midfield, Archie Gemmill consistently gave a 100 per cent performance.

CHARLIE GEORGE

Charlie had a touch of individualism that set him apart from a lot of other players in the 1970s. His long hair and rebellious nature combined with a natural talent to make him the big crowd-pleaser of the fine Arsenal side that achieved the League and FA Cup double in 1971. Coming from Islington, he was the local hero at Highbury and his little touches of magic provided the appeal in a team that was otherwise essentially well organised and disciplined. In those days he was the attacking midfield player behind two very accomplished front strikers – John Radford and Ray Kennedy.

There's no doubt that he had a wonderful ability, if a slightly impetuous nature that would sometimes get him into trouble with referees. He had good vision, tight control and was capable of hitting a superb long pass. He was an explosive player who scored vital goals. Perhaps his most notable came in extra time in 1971 in the FA Cup final against Liverpool at Wembley. He hit a super shot from outside the box to give Arsenal a 2–1

Charlie George (striker)
Islington 10.10.50
Arsenal, Derby County, Southampton, Nottingham Forest
England – 1

Still much loved at Highbury, Charlie is remembered for his super goals during Arsenal's double season of 1971 – particularly the FA Cup-winner against Liverpool at Wembley.

lead and then lay prostrate on the pitch with his arms outstretched. Arsenal had beaten Spurs to win the First Division title five days earlier and Charlie's goal secured the double.

At times he could be a frustrating player with a temptation to over-elaborate but when the ball arrived at his feet a buzz would invariably go round the ground because the crowd knew that he could turn a match with a single piece of brilliance. He didn't go out of his way to endear himself to the game's establishment but it says much for his contribution at Arsenal that after a mere five years in the first team he is still remembered at Highbury with great affection.

Arsenal sold him to Derby in 1975 and, for me, his most exciting years as a player were in the role of a front striker at the Baseball Ground. He scored 34 goals in 100 League games during a three year spell with Derby and it was while at the Baseball Ground that he won his only England cap. He played in the 1–1 draw against Eire at Wembley in September 1976. He was substituted during the match by Gordon Hill and that was the end of his international career.

Don Revie was manager and I was a regular in the team and could not understand why a player of Charlie's undeniable talent didn't get more opportunities on the international stage. Sadly, he suffered a bad knee injury while at Derby and that certainly didn't help his prospects as far as international football was concerned. No one quite realised the full implications of the injury and Southampton even paid Derby £400,000 to take Charlie to the Dell in 1978. He played just 22 games for them before going to Nottingham Forest on loan. I always felt that it was a shame that Charlie, a player blessed with such wonderful skills, never reached the heights that his talent warranted.

ALAN GILZEAN

Alan Gilzean was an unorthodox striker, but one of the finest touch players I've seen in the British game since the war. His touch was both delicate and deadly and he was a thrilling player to watch, racing to the near post to meet a cross with a perfect glancing header. But to see him in a crowded room full of strangers you would never have guessed that he was a professional footballer. He had a slight, stooping stature and thinning hair and, off the field, he was not the most glamorous of dressers among the Tottenham superstars of the 1960s.

Bill Nicholson, the Spurs manager, wasn't interested in his sartorial elegance when he paid Dundee £72,000 for Alan in 1964. That year John White had died, Danny Blanchflower and Terry Medwin had retired and Terry Dyson and Les Allen had moved to new clubs. The great double side of 1961 was breaking up and Nicholson began rebuilding the team by signing Gilzean from Dundee, Pat Jennings from Watford and Cyril Knowles from Middlesbrough. Gilzean signed for Spurs even though Sunderland had made him a better offer. Nicholson revealed some time after the signing that he had accidentally misled Gilzean over some financial matters during the contractual negotiations. Apparently, Gilzean knew he was being misled, but so wanted to join Spurs that he signed anyway, spurning Sunderland's better offer. As was typical of Gilzean, he never complained, but when Nicholson realised that he had made a mistake, he gave Alan a wage rise.

'Gilly' repaid his manager a thousandfold. He spent nine years at White Hart Lane, becoming a firm favourite with the crowd and scoring 83 goals in 350 games for the club. He was not a big, muscular centre forward like his predecessor at Tottenham, Bobby Smith; nor was he the neat busy striker so typical of the Scottish game. He was rather an unusual striker in my opinion, blessed with a superb creative touch that perfectly comp- lemented two very different strike partners – first Jimmy Greaves and then Martin Chivers.

Gilly's heading ability was one of the main features of his game. He didn't meet the ball with powerful, booming headers like Smith or Chivers, instead he applied a little glancing touch allowing the ball to skim off the top of his head. He headed a lot of goals himself but set up many more for others with his delicate headed passes. The secret of this was his timing. He timed his runs to the near post and his jumps for the ball to the second. As a midfield player myself I know the value of being aware of what's going on around you, especially when you are under pressure and trying to make the right pass. Gilzean was a striker with a midfield player's awareness; when he was receiving the ball he didn't have to look up before laying it off. He invariably knew the positions that his team-mates had taken up.

I enjoyed playing against him, but I got even more enjoyment from watching him as he was a thrilling, spontaneous player who should have

Alan Gilzean (striker)
Perth 22.10.38
Dundee United, Tottenham
Hotspur
Scotland – 22

won far more than 22 Scottish caps. Nicholson thought the world of Gilzean because he didn't moan, he took criticism in the right spirit and was trustworthy and likeable. Away from football he was something of a lone wolf; in the dressing room he was quiet and unaggressive and used to soak his boots in hot water to soften them up before every match.

It was a tribute to his fitness that he was still playing for Tottenham at the age of 36. When he retired in 1973 he had played for Spurs in the 1967 FA Cup final, the 1972 UEFA Cup final and two Football League Cup finals. Fifteen years after retiring his son Ian joined Tottenham as a trainee.

Spurs v Crystal Palace, 1971. Few players have been as deadly in the air as Tottenham's Alan Gilzean (right) at the peak of his career.

EDDIE GRAY

I attended a dinner with Eddie Gray a couple of years ago and when he was introduced to the guests I was staggered to learn that he had won only 12 caps for Scotland. At the end of the dinner I asked Eddie if it was true that he had played just a dozen times for his country and he said it was. It was only then that I realised how badly his career had been marred by injuries. It was a great shame because in my opinion he has been one of the purest and most dynamic talents in the game since the war.

When I was mulling over which names to include in my favourite 100, Eddie's was one of the very first on my list. I always found him a very exciting player to watch and when you are talking about great players their entertainment value is an important consideration. His dribbling, his close control at speed and his ability to go past defenders almost put him into a class of his own in my opinion. He had all the skills of the classic winger, but was also able to work back and cover his defence and fill the role of the modern midfield man. But it was when he had the ball at his feet that he was the most devastating.

I think we saw his true worth in the 1970 FA Cup final when Don Revie's powerful Leeds side, who finished second in the League championship that season, faced Chelsea at Wembley. No one remembers that final more vividly than David Webb. At Wembley Webb, a rugged and uncompromising defender, played at right back and was roasted by Gray. After 90 minutes the crowd was wondering how Chelsea had managed to keep going and secure a 2–2 draw and a replay. As Gray had been so outstanding in the first game the Chelsea manager, Dave Sexton, decied to make changes for the replay at Old Trafford. Webb switched to centre-back and Sexton paid Gray the compliment of detailing Ron 'Chopper' Harris to mark the Leeds winger. Gray had another good game but was not nearly so efficient against Harris; Webb at least had the satisfaction of heading the winning goal.

Eddie had a slightly round-shouldered stance, which in some ways helped him to shield the ball and he had all the tricks of the finest wingers – the drags back, rolling the ball under his feet and dummies. He teased and toyed with his markers and could hit crosses with stunning accuracy. For me he was the jewel in a slightly dour, though highly effective, Leeds team and it was a great shame that his catalogue of injuries prevented him playing more often for Scotland.

He made his debut for Leeds in 1966, had four seasons with them averaging around 30 matches a season and then, in the five years following the 1970 FA Cup final, averaged only 15 games a season. In total he spent 20 years on the Leeds United playing staff and in 1972 was joined there by his younger brother Frank who became a very successful defender.

For me Eddie was one of the game's great crowd-pleasers; he is the sort of player you would gladly pay to watch and he certainly drew the fans

Eddie Gray MBE (winger)
Glasgow 17.1.48
Leeds United
Scotland – 12

The jewel in the crown. Crowd-pleaser Eddie Gray stood out in a clinically efficient Leeds United side.

through the turnstiles. The skills he showed in the 1970s are what we should be showing to youngsters in coaching films today. When he finished playing he became manager at Elland Road, though he couldn't repeat the success of the Don Revie era. He was later manager at Rochdale.

JIMMY GREAVES

Jimmy burst into the headlines with Chelsea in the mid-1950s at a time when the club was producing a string of good young players. His touch and instinct in the penalty box were apparent from the moment he scored on his League debut against Tottenham. In a wonderful career he was to top the First Division goalscoring charts six times as he became widely acknowledged as the most prolific goalscoring machine of modern times.

I remember watching him when I was a youngster and the thing that formed a lasting impression with me was his ability to beat goalkeepers without striking the ball hard. Accuracy and composure in tight situations were the key elements in his game. He was always in the right position, he invariably placed his shots and his ability to disguise the direction of his shooting frequently wrong-footed the goalkeeper. In my opinion he was the most clinical finisher of the last 25 years. People say that he wouldn't have been able to play in today's game, but I would totally disagree with that. Players with Jimmy's ability will always score goals and will adapt to the circumstances and demands made on them.

Like so many great strikers, Jim relied on a good service in much the same way that Gary Lineker does today. The fact that he played in the great Spurs side of the early 1960s – they paid £99,999 to AC Milan for him because the manager Bill Nicholson refused to make him the first £100,000 player – obviously enhanced his reputation. One manager, though, who had doubts about Jim's contribution to the team play was Alf Ramsey, who controversially left him out of England's 1966 World Cup winning team – that still rankles with Jim. Nonetheless, he played 57 times for his country, scoring 44 goals. Only Bobby Charlton has scored more for England since the war.

Jimmy Greaves (striker)
East Ham 20.2.40
Chelsea, AC Milan,
Tottenham Hotspur, West
Ham United
England – 57

Spurs' new acquisition, Jimmy Greaves, poses for the camera a few hours after his return to English football.

Ramsey saw Greaves purely as a goalscorer who made no other significant contribution to the team. He wasn't renowned for his heading ability or his work-rate and he wasn't the bravest of players but his balance, cunning and accuracy in front of the goal more than compensated for that. Jim had the pace and ability to dart past defenders in tight situations and the television companies frequently reel out a marvellous piece of old film of an electrifying run against Manchester United when he picked up the ball on the halfway line, wriggled through the United defence and finally walked round the goalkeeper. It was vintage Greaves.

I was fortunate enough to play with him as he was finishing his career at West Ham. They weren't the best years of his career; Jim always says that if you ask Chelsea supporters which were his best years they will say those at Chelsea and if you ask Spurs supporters they will say those at Spurs, but if you ask West Ham supporters they will say those at Chelsea or Spurs! West Ham signed him in 1970 in an exchange deal involving Martin Peters and although Jim hadn't lost his skill, his appetite was waning. In his last months with us he was playing on the left side of midfield which was a terrible waste as he was one of those players who really only came to life in the opposing penalty area.

He was always a chirpy, Cockney character and as a youngster in the West Ham side I can recall no hint then of the problems that were to engulf his private life. The fact that he was to emerge from those problems and establish himself as a household name in a completely different field – that of television – is a testimony to his strength of character. I think he's one of the few players who will stand the test of time. In years to come people will still be making comparisons with the incomparable Jimmy Greaves.

TONY GREEN

In November 1973 Tony Green announced that because of a worsening knee problem he was retiring from the professional game at the age of 27 on medical advice. It was a shattering blow for Tony because at one time it looked as though he could become one of the truly great players of the post-war era. I used to love watching him and his injury brought home to me the precarious nature of professional football as a living.

Tony was a Glasgow boy who played 70 games for Albion Rovers before Blackpool, who had just been relegated to Division Two, paid £12,000 for him in May 1967. He quickly settled to the pace and commitment of the English game and, although I was aware of him, it wasn't until I went to Blackpool and watched him play against West Ham that I really appreciated the full range of his talents. I travelled with the team to Bloomfield Road in January 1971 hoping to play that day particularly because it was an FA Cup third round tie.

When we got into the dressing room I was disappointed to discover that I wasn't in the side but, after watching from the stand for 90 minutes, I was quite relieved not to have been involved because Blackpool trounced us 4–0. The man who did the damage was Tony Green; he slaughtered us almost single-handedly. He scored twice, but that was just the icing on the cake, so to speak. We simply couldn't contain him and it was then that I thought 'What a great little player'.

Tony's balance and pace destroyed us on the frosty surface that afternoon. It was one of the shock results of the third round and it had far reaching repercussions because four of our players – Bobby Moore, Jimmy Greaves, Clyde Best and Brian Dear – had been spotted in former boxer Brian London's night club the evening before the game. When the story leaked out it received front page coverage; all four players were fined and Bobby was stripped of the club captaincy. It soured his relationship with the manager at the time, Ron Greenwood, and in many ways was the beginning of the end of his career at Upton Park.

The season before, Green had helped Blackpool to finish runners-up in Division Two and, once he was playing football with the élite of the First Division, it was inevitable that he would gain international recognition. Scotland chose him to make his debut against Belgium in 1971 and that, plus his part in the destruction of West Ham in the FA Cup, began to attract the attention of bigger clubs. He had won six Scotland caps by the time he moved to Newcastle in October 1971 for a fee of £140,000. He seemed destined to become one of the greats: a slim, lightweight attacking midfield player, he slipped comfortably into the Newcastle side of Macdonald, Tudor, Hibbitt and company. He played 27 League games for Newcastle that season and, somewhat ironically, was in the side which was knocked out of the FA Cup by Hereford, then a non-League side, in the third round. It was exactly a year since he had caused West Ham similar embarrassment

Tony Green (midfield)
Glasgow 3.10.46
Albion Rovers, Blackpool,
Newcastle United
Scotland – 6

Tony Green, the star of the Blackpool side that knocked West Ham out of the FA Cup in 1971.

but, as it happened, West Ham then beat Hereford in round four.

Sadly, that was his last FA Cup tie. He started the following season full of optimism, jinking past defenders and setting up chances for Macdonald. He seemed to skim across the surface when he ran, as if the ball were tied to his boots. His control and balance were so good that defenders had little opportunity to tackle him, but one tackle was enough to finish his career. It came at Crystal Palace in September 1972 – the last match he ever played. He had two knee operations, but just over a year later he announced his retirement. He eventually returned to Blackpool where he settled down as a schoolmaster, teaching maths and physical education.

ALAN HANSEN

If there was ever a youngster who was going to make a name for himself, it had to be Alan Hansen. Not only was he a brilliant, multi-talented sportsman, but he was also an above-average scholar. When he left Lornshill Academy in his home town of Alloa he had seven O level GCEs and four A levels, including a pass in Latin. As a teenager he played for Scotland at golf — he had a two handicap at 18 — volleyball and squash but it was as a soccer player that he really excelled. A naturally gifted player, he couldn't have chosen a better football education than the one he has received at Anfield. He has repaid them a thousand times and I often feel that he has not been given the credit he deserves. Of course, they acknowledge his vast contribution at Anfield but, beyond that, I feel he has struggled for recognition.

Alan Hansen (centre back)
Alloa 13.6.55
Partick Thistle, Liverpool
Scotland — 26

Danny Blanchflower, with Tottenham, and Frank McLintock, with Arsenal, are the only other two captains to have led their teams to the fabled League and FA Cup double this century and they were swamped with adulation. The praise for Hansen seemed lukewarm by contrast but perhaps that's because we are now so used to seeing Liverpool capture the season's silverware. Hansen's career has been one of almost unrivalled achievement since he joined Liverpool from Partick Thistle in May 1977. He'd had a trial with Liverpool at the age of 15 and they had turned him down — his father still has the letter of rejection. But when he was 21 Liverpool changed their minds and Bob Paisley was the manager who paid £100,000 for him.

By this time he had played 100 games for Partick and was a tall, coltish, leggy defender who gave the appearance of being a little too casual. Liverpool centre backs before him had been hard, uncompromising characters of the Ron Yeats, Willie Stevenson, Tommy Smith type; Hansen didn't fit into that physical category at all. He has never been anything but lean and calm with a long stride that quickly overtakes attackers or carries him with ease deep into enemy positions. In fact, his game is all about skill, subtlety, anticipation — almost delicacy. His secret is that he always seems to have time in tight situations. He is the defender with the clearest head in the most difficult moments and it's his awareness and good close control that buys him the time to get out of trouble. His composure on the ball reminds me in many ways of some of the great Brazilian defenders who were almost leisurely in playing themselves out of trouble.

His surges from deep positions to create attacking openings and throw the opposition into confusion have played a major role in Liverpool's successes over the years. He times his runs to perfection and knows when to release the ball — a knack not all centre backs have mastered. Watching him play one day it occurred to me that he must have an analytical sort of mind because, having weighed up a situation, he invariably makes the right judgment. Perhaps it has something to do with his Scottish education.

His partnership with Mark Lawrenson, an outstanding player in his own right who moved to Anfield from Brighton a few months after Hansen, probably gave Liverpool one of the shrewdest, coolest centre-back pairings in European football since the war. There must have been a few occasions over the years in big European matches when opposing centre forwards have looked across at Hansen and envisaged an easy match. But his clean cut, boyish looks disguise a very positive, proud and intimidating personality. He has, in fact, all the qualities required of a team captain and it was no surprise to me when player–manager Kenny Dalglish appointed him to that post in 1985. Alan's greatest achievement as captain was to lead Liverpool to the double the following season.

That was his first FA Cup triumph, but his sixth League championship medal. He won his seventh championship medal in his testimonial season of 1987–88. He has also played in three European Cup winning teams and in four League/Milk Cup winning sides. Alan is a player of such experience, skill and tenacity, that it has always puzzled me why the Scotland team didn't make more use of him. I was quite baffled when the Scots left him out of their squad of 22 for the 1986 World Cup in Mexico. He made his international debut in 1979 and played in the 1982 World Cup in Spain but, five years later when he was 32 and still a vital cog in the Liverpool machine, he had played a total of just 26 times for his country.

Alan Hansen on the rampage at Coventry City in 1987. His anticipation, composure and ball-control have established him as an outstanding defender.

COLIN HARVEY

I remember going to Goodison Park for a Milk Cup replay against Everton in 1983–84 and being rather surprised to hear so much talk and speculation about the future of their manager, Howard Kendall. Everton had a few problems at the time, but I didn't realise that the situation was quite so delicate as far as Howard's future was concerned. The game took place in the December of that season when Everton were seventeenth in the table; they beat us 2–0 in extra time and that win was really the start of Everton's

Colin Harvey (midfield)
Liverpool 16.11.44
Everton, Sheffield Wednesday
England – 1

Colin Harvey was the stabilising influence in the midfield trio that was instrumental in Everton's Championship triumph in 1970.

revival. It was also around that time that Howard upgraded Colin Harvey from reserve team coach to first team coach. Colin and Howard had formed a great playing partnership with Everton and were about to do the same at managerial level. That season Everton went on to win the FA Cup, lose the Milk Cup final to Liverpool at Wembley and finish seventh in the First Division.

It's interesting that Harvey, Kendall and Alan Ball, who formed such an impressive midfield in the Everton championship winning team of 1970, have all established themselves since at the top level of management and coaching. Of the three, Colin was the least likely to capture the headlines as a player. For a start he was a local Liverpool boy who hadn't cost Everton a fee, as Ball and Kendall had, and as a player he didn't catch the eye like the other two did. But Colin was an outstanding team player – conscientious rather than spectacular – and I remember him well because he was one of the most difficult opponents I ever faced. He always made life difficult for me because of his attitude and commitment. Every good team has a player like Colin, although their contribution is often ignored by those on the terraces.

He had a sound, all-round game, was quick and particularly strong in the tackle, in fact he was probably the backbone of Everton's championship winning team in 1970. He was considered good enough to play for England, but won only one cap, in a game against Malta in a 1–0 victory in 1970–71. Sadly, injuries caused him problems late in his career and he was only 31 when he finished playing with Sheffield Wednesday in 1975. He later had a hip replacement operation, but that has never stopped him from playing a full role in Everton's training programmes.

As a player I would liken him to Peter Reid in that he was a vital part of the side who never quite got the plaudits his contribution deserved. He was the sort of player all managers love to have in their team. When Kendall left Goodison Park to join Athletic Bilbao in the summer of 1987 I wasn't in the least surprised that Everton decided to upgrade Harvey once again and make him manager. He had shown he had all the necessary qualities for the job and one of his first moves impressed me no end – he appointed Peter Reid to the coaching staff.

JOHNNY HAYNES

I think Johnny Haynes will always be remembered as the game's first £100 a week footballer though I fancy he would prefer to be remembered for the quality of his football as he certainly ranks among the outstanding post-war inside forwards. He was one of the players who made me realise as a youngster that nothing was quite so important as being able to pass accurately. He had many attributes but his long through ball was widely acknowledged as his greatest strength. I think Fulham deserve a lot of credit for keeping such a talented and sought-after player at Craven Cottage. He was a schoolboy prodigy before signing for the club but it was their decision to make him the first £100 a week player — an enormous sum in those days — that persuaded him to stay when he could have moved abroad.

John made his first team debut in 1952 at the age of 17 and played nearly 600 League games for the club before leaving to join Durban City in South Africa in 1970. He was lucky enough to play for Fulham at a time when they were one of the big names in the game, as much for their show business connections as for their achievements on the field. Tommy Trinder, the comedian, was the chairman, and they had great characters on the field like 'Tosh' Chamberlain and Jimmy Hill. Haynes was regarded as the creative impetus in the side. His vision, long passing and leadership ability were qualities that fuelled Fulham's swashbuckling, attacking style. He became renowned for the Haynes reverse pass which enabled him to run in one direction and pass in the opposite direction — a ploy that frequently wrong-footed defenders. He was predominantly right footed but could switch play with either foot and when he passed to a team-mate he expected the pass to get there. He could be rather theatrical on the field and there were times when he showed his irritation with team-mates who had failed to anticipate a pass.

Bobby Robson, who played alongside Haynes long before his days as England team manager, often gives Haynes lavish credit for his passing, adding 'But I did all his running, of course'. It sounds to me as though Johnny Haynes was a player after my own heart! When Fulham's attacks broke down he would invariably stroll back in frustration, with no thought of chasing back and getting in a tackle. He felt that his particular contribution wasn't necessary until Fulham were again in possession of the ball. The days of the midfield player who worked back to help out his defence were still in the future.

Style was important to John; as well as being very talented he was always perfectly groomed — he appeared regularly in the Brylcream advertisements — and he was one of the first footballing superstars to employ an agent. He enjoyed a wonderful career, playing 56 times for England following international appearances at every level other than amateur. Sadly, a car injury in 1962 finished his international career though he was able to continue helping out in Fulham's regular battle against relegation.

Johnny Haynes (midfield)
Edmonton 17.10.34
Fulham
England — 56

Had he gone to a bigger club I'm sure he would have retired with several of the game's major domestic trophies in his possession. He came close to playing in the FA Cup final in 1958 when Fulham faced Manchester United in the semi-finals shortly after the Munich air disaster. Being a Londoner I leaned towards Fulham but there was a great and natural well of sympathy at that time for United. Fulham lost 5–3 in a replay and so Haynes missed his chance of an FA Cup final medal.

If Johnny had been playing today the chances are that he would eventually have found his way to one of the big glamour clubs like Liverpool, Manchester United or Arsenal. These days, as clubs are allowed to keep all their receipts from home League matches, the well-supported teams make the most money and, inevitably, are able to invest in the best players. When John was playing the visiting clubs took a share of the gate money at places like Anfield, Old Trafford and Highbury. The money was then more evenly spread throughout the League, enabling smaller clubs like Fulham to hold on to their star players. That apart, I think John enjoyed the family atmosphere at Craven Cottage where he was a big fish in one of the First Division's smaller ponds.

Swashbuckling inside forward Johnny Haynes was the first £100-a-week footballer and one of the game's earliest superstars.

GLENN HODDLE

I think there has probably been more debate about the merits of Glenn Hoddle than of any other player in the English game over the last 10 to 15 years. There are those who can't find enough superlatives to describe him and others who feel that his remarkable talent has been wasted. Beauty is in the eyes of the beholder and it all depends on what type of player you enjoy watching. There is no doubt in my mind that he is as gifted a footballer as I've seen since George Best drifted out of the game. His touch on the ball is quite brilliant and when I worked with him closely during England training sessions I saw him mesmerise team-mates with his skills. There have been times when I've been amazed at what he has been able to achieve on the training pitch. He's equally adept with both feet and is easily the best two footed player of his generation which, in itself, makes him a rarity. There is much about his game that reminds me of the great South American players – the perfect weight he places on a pass, the precision with which he kills a ball and ensures it doesn't bounce away from him, and his marvellous ability to pull the ball down almost from shoulder height with either foot.

His critics' main gripe is that he disappears from games for long periods; they argue that he doesn't involve himself for the full 90 minutes. I must say that I have seen him play in games where he has taken a back seat for far too long but, on other days, I've seen him transform a match with one or two moments of individual brilliance. Perhaps there is a price to pay for such outstanding talent. If there is, then in Hoddle's case the team he plays for should be happy to pay it. My chief criticism of him would be that he doesn't run with the ball as much as he could. I've seen him dribble past defenders with ease in training but for some reason he has always seemed reluctant to take on defenders in full stride during matches. On the other hand, his greatest strength is unquestionably his long passing and his ability to switch the point of attack so devastatingly.

Glenn's long shooting has always been impressive and early in his career with Tottenham he was quite happy to thunder 25-yard drives at the opposing goalkeeper. He got his fair share of goals, too – 19 in the League in 1979–80 – but more recently he's taken to chipping his shots over the goalkeeper and although this can bring the crowd to their feet I don't think it produces so many goals. Occasionally I felt a little sorry for him because of all the argument he provoked quite unwittingly, especially when he was trying to establish himself in the England side. Ron Greenwood gave him his debut against Bulgaria in 1979 where he scored with a long range shot, but it probably took him five more years before he became a fixture in the side. Every good professional wants to be a regular player in the England side but, according to many sections of the media, Glenn always seemed to be on trial when he was selected. He always had to justify his place and that must have become a bit tiresome for him.

Glenn Hoddle (midfield)
Hayes 27.10.57
Tottenham Hotspur, Monaco
England – 53

Glenn Hoddle is one of the most talked-about players of the 1980s. Love him or hate him — and everyone has an opinion — he is capable of transforming a match with a moment of individual brilliance.

Hoddle spent 15 glorious years at White Hart Lane and had a great final season in 1986–87 before accepting a £1 million contract to play for Monaco in the French League for three years. In his last season at Spurs he gave full value for 90 minutes in every game I saw, though he must have been disappointed with his performance in the FA Cup final against Coventry. It was to be his farewell game and Coventry spoiled his day by marking him tightly and winning the match. He had to learn to come to terms with close marking in the French League but such is his talent that I think he will overcome all obstacles on the Continent. His game is suited to Continental football and had I been in the same situation and had the opportunity arisen, I'm sure I would have gone to play abroad long before I was 29. In his first season with Monaco, playing alongside England team-mate Mark Hateley, he helped them win the French League.

JOHN HOLLINS

John gets into my top 100 because of his honesty, his attitude and his enthusiasm. As much as anything else, he was a player who inspired those around him with his relentless pursuit of lost causes – he never knew when to give up. Dave Sexton, who was his manager at Chelsea, once told me that he would never consider dropping John just because of one poor game because he knew that in the next match he would run until he dropped in order to compensate. He was that type of player.

John was one of a stream of good young players to emerge from the Stamford Bridge assembly line. He was neat and precise and made an impression at Chelsea in the early 1960s. He won an England cap against Spain in 1967 (this was slightly unusual because his brother Dave was already an international goalkeeper with Wales) and helped Chelsea to win the FA Cup in a memorable replayed final against Leeds United in 1970 and the European Cup-winners' Cup the following year.

John Hollins MBE (midfield)
Guildford 16.7.46
Chelsea, Queen's Park Rangers, Arsenal
England – 1

A reliable and diligent performer, John Hollins' reputation, on and off the field, was impeccable.

He was probably one of the best strikers·of a dead ball that I've ever played with or against; he could hit a free kick 50 or 60 yards and it would drop perfectly at the feet of a team-mate. He was also an excellent penalty taker. He was alert, deceptively quick and a tigerish tackler. He was also a very good organiser and it was these qualities which helped him through the last years of his playing career as a right back with Arsenal. That he was as fit in his mid-30s as he had been in his mid-20s says a lot about the way he looked after himself. He was a great professional both on and off the field, with great self-confidence, and the fact that he survived a traumatic period in his early days as manager at Chelsea speaks volumes for his character.

It was no surprise when John went into management. He had a spotless reputation as a player and a bubbly, outgoing personality that seemed to draw out the best in those around him. I have never played in the same team as John, but I can imagine that he was a tremendous asset in the dressing room before a big match. I don't think I've ever seen him without a smile on his face. He always reserved his biggest smile for those occasions when he hit a rocket-like right foot shot into the top of the net from 30 yards. He didn't do that very often, but when he did it certainly brought the crowd to their feet.

Unfortunately for John, problems were never far from the surface at Stamford Bridge during his management reign. They came to a head for him in the 1987–88 season. Chelsea made a reasonable start to the season, but the team lost form and confidence and was badly hit by injuries, and John, a naturally ebullient personality, became tense and wary. I think the media attention to life at Stamford Bridge put him under further pressure and when chairman Ken Bates appointed Bobby Campbell as first team coach, John felt that it was time to leave. It was a sad and traumatic end to a 20-year career as player, coach and manager at Chelsea. He left with handsome compensation though; his memories of nearly 600 first team games and a self-belief that I was sure would help him to re-establish himself in the game. I'm confident that he'll be a better manager for the experience.

ALAN HUDSON

I always associate Alan Hudson with Peter Osgood, because they were two similarly outstanding players who formed the creative heart of a very fine Chelsea side under Dave Sexton's management in the mid-1970s. Alan was a short-passing player with a deft first touch and watching him reminded me of some of the old Spurs teams that specialized in the push and run

Alan Hudson (midfield)
Chelsea 21.6.51
Chelsea, Stoke City, Arsenal
England – 2

Alan Hudson, a talented and colourful member of manager Dave Sexton's glamorous Chelsea side of the mid-1970s.

technique; he was a player out of that mould. He liked to collect the ball from the back four, play it forward, take the return and start again. He had great vision and awareness and was predominantly right footed. He rarely used his left foot but he appeared to possess what I can describe only as a revolving knee cap which allowed him to turn in the tightest of situations, keeping the ball on his right foot all the time. To be so one footed would be considered a weakness by some, but he could jink past a defender on both sides, using either the inside or the outside of his right foot.

Hudson was just a lad living in the old prefabs near Stamford Bridge when he got into the Chelsea first team in 1968, where he was an immediate success and looked to be one of the most promising youngsters of his generation. As far as ability was concerned, he was as gifted as any midfield player of that time and, had his attitude been a little more mature, he could have reached far greater heights. He had a short spell in the England squad, winning two caps under Don Revie during his three years at Stoke.

Alan was a bit of a rebel – one of the characters who seemed to populate the game during the 1970s. He was frequently in the headlines – not always for praiseworthy reasons – and seemed to enjoy the King's Road atmosphere that enveloped the Chelsea team. They were a very glamorous side and he was one of the stars. He was probably too young to handle the fame that was thrust upon him and I suspect that he sometimes fell into the wrong company. He didn't always lead the life that a professional should or that a manager would want him to lead. He and Peter Osgood left Stamford Bridge within months of each other after a series of rows with the manager; it was the beginning of the end of Chelsea's great years.

It was significant that he probably played the best football of his career during his three years at Stoke, where he came under the influence of Geoff Hurst, by then a mature and vastly experienced player who was able to restore a sense of perspective to Hudson's career. Alan went to live with Geoff and his wife Judith in their big house in the countryside around Stoke where the temptations were fewer and his game inevitably benefited. He was quite superb during that period of his career and he never reached the same heights when he returned to London to play for Arsenal. For all his faults, he was a great entertainer when he had the ball at his feet – the sort of player I would gladly pay to watch.

EMLYN HUGHES

Emlyn was the son of a Welsh rugby league star who, wisely in my opinion, decided that the round ball game was more suited to his talents. He enjoyed 13 enormously successful seasons with Liverpool where he won just about every honour available in the game. He was born in Barrow and began his professional career with Blackpool in September 1964. Three years later Bill Shankly spotted his potential and paid £65,000 to take him to Anfield. At Liverpool he became known as 'Crazy Horse' because of his many forays

Emlyn Hughes OBE (full back)
Barrow 28.8.47
Blackpool, Liverpool,
Wolverhampton Wanderers,
Rotherham United, Hull City,
Swansea City
England – 62

Emlyn 'Crazy Horse' Hughes, a versatile, rampaging defender and an influential figure on the field during his successful years with Liverpool and England.

121

from deep defensive positions into enemy territory. I always felt that his personality, which was later to earn him a nationwide reputation as a television celebrity, was the key to his game. He was a chatterbox, an enthusiast, a bubbly, likeable character – and all these elements of his make-up would become apparent during the 90 minutes of a match.

The Anfield crowd loved him and when those long legs carried him on one of his swirling runs down the left flank you could sense them willing him forward. He was a versatile player who could appear at full back, centre back or in midfield. I remember that most of the games he played for Liverpool were at left back – even though he was predominantly right footed – but his attacking instincts meant that he was frequently foraging for the ball in midfield. The fact that he was right footed, of course, often meant that when he got into attacking situations on the left flank he had to turn inside onto his stronger right foot to cross the ball. It never seemed to worry him – or Liverpool for that matter.

Beneath the infectious personality was a very ambitious and determined player. He was consistent, committed, a strong tackler and a demanding captain for both Liverpool and England. He played 62 times for England in an 11-year international career and had phenomenal success at club level with Liverpool, winning four League championship medals and playing in two European Cup winning teams. He was voted Footballer of the Year in 1978.

When he eventually left Liverpool and joined Wolves in August 1979 the only club trophy he was still hoping to add to his collection was the League Cup which, remarkably, Wolves won, beating Nottingham Forest in the final that season. He began to suffer with knee trouble at Wolves and finished his playing career in the lower divisions with Rotherham, Hull and Swansea but, at his peak, he was the sort of player every manager would like to send out on a Saturday afternoon.

NORMAN HUNTER

I can almost hear the gasps of astonishment. Norman was not the most delicate of defenders and many of you may consider him to be a surprising choice. He was termed a 'hatchet man' and one of the most popular banners among the Leeds United followers in the 1970s was the one that read 'Norman Bites Yer Legs'. He was certainly a formidable tackler and he challenged for the ball as though his life depended on it. His attitude was quite daunting; it was as if he regarded being beaten as a personal affront, something to be remembered and later rectified. There is no doubt that occasionally his tackling went beyond the boundaries of fair play but, compared to many of the other hard men of the time – Tommy Smith, Nobby Stiles and Peter Storey come to mind – Norman had quite a high degree of skill that went largely unnoticed by the public. His aggressive reputation flourished and blossomed in the uncompromising Leeds team of

Norman Hunter (centre back)
Middlesbrough 29.10.43
Leeds United, Bristol City,
Barnsley
England – 28

Manchester United's Stuart Pearson on the receiving end of a typically ferocious Norman Hunter challenge. Hunter was perhaps the most efficient left footed tackler of the 1970s.

the Don Revie era but for me, players like Allan Clarke and Johnny Giles had a ruthless streak in them that made them altogether more dangerous than Norman.

Tall, cool and lean, Norman was largely left footed, but he could use the ball stylishly. A Middlesbrough lad, he joined Leeds in 1960 and worked his way diligently through the Elland Road youth scheme before breaking into the first team in 1962. When he helped the club to win the Second Division championship in 1964 it was obvious that he would be a key defender in the emergence of a very fine team. Under Revie's astute management, Norman played a big part in providing Leeds with the foundations for their sustained assault on all the major honours in the 1970s. In a 15-year career of 600 games with Leeds, Norman helped them to win the First Division title (twice), the Second Division title, the FA Cup, League Cup and the old Inter Cities Fairs Cup and he could have won so much more. Much to Revie's chagrin, Leeds finished runners-up more often than they finished winners. During Revie's reign, Leeds finished First Division runners-up four times and were unsuccessful FA Cup finalists on three occasions. I felt at the time that this led to a little bitterness among some of the Leeds players which I think was sometimes apparent in their play. Revie made sure that they made the most of their triumphs though.

Leeds needed one point from their final game at Anfield – from where Liverpool had dominated the 1960s – in order to win the League title for the first time in 1969. The match was a thunderous affair although no goals were scored, and at the end Revie led his champions to the Leeds fans and then to the masses of Liverpool fans in the Kop. Sullen silence greeted Hunter, Bremner, Giles and company until the players began to raise their arms in salute. Like rolling thunder, a monstrous roar swelled and boomed down from the terraces to greet the new champions of England.

But Leeds could never be ranked among the most popular champions. They were determined, disciplined, competitive and, with players like Hunter and Jack Charlton in defence and Giles and Bremner in midfield, almost impossible to beat. Leeds' secret at that time was that they kept possession and rarely gave the ball away. Even at the back they played the ball so as to ensure they retained possession. Norman's distribution was excellent; he wasn't a hit and hoof man. His passing was accurate and his timing was impeccable. Unfortunately his timing let him down once with disastrous consequences.

Many people will remember the World Cup qualifying tie against Poland in 1973 when Sir Alf Ramsey picked Norman instead of the England captain and my West Ham team-mate Bobby Moore. England had to win that match in order to qualify for the World Cup finals in West Germany and Norman made a crucial error in timing a tackle, allowing the little Pole, Lato, to scurry past him down the wing and set up a goal for Domarski. The match ended 1–1 and England failed to qualify. On any other occasion Norman would have put the ball and Lato into the first row of the spectator seating, but this time Norman tried to play his way out of trouble. Perhaps he felt it was the thing to do because he was in the side instead of the more refined Moore. Whatever the reason, the badly timed tackle was a mistake that he has never been allowed to forget.

I think Norman was good enough to have won far more than 28 England caps had it not been for Moore's consistency. Norman came into the side just after the World Cup triumph in 1966 and was still a faithful member of the squad 10 years later when his former Leeds manager, Revie, was in charge.

In my opinion Norman was a much better player than people gave him credit for. He was hard, there's no doubt about that, but he wasn't malicious and he had a sense of humour. Having chopped down an opponent he had a habit of raising his arms in mock surprise and horror as if to say, 'Could I have done that?'. He left Leeds in 1976 and had three seasons at Bristol City, where he was still sticking out a leg to slow down opposing strikers as they turned away from him. He returned to Yorkshire with Barnsley in 1979 as player–manager and led them to promotion from Division Three in 1981. Four years later he became manager of Rotherham but in December 1987, after a string of bad results, he suffered the fate of so many managers and was sacked. Within two months his old Leeds team-mate Billy Bremner, manager at Elland Road, had offered him a coaching job on the staff.

GEOFF HURST

Geoff Hurst MBE (striker)
Ashton-under-Lyne 8.12.41
West Ham United, Stoke City,
West Bromwich Albion
England – 49

The familiar cheek-blowing pose
of Geoff Hurst, who carved his
name in the annals of soccer
history with his hat trick in the
1966 World Cup final against
West Germany.

Geoff started at West Ham as a wing half of modest potential and must owe a lot of what unfolded during his magnificent career to Ron Greenwood. It was the former West Ham and England manager who had the greatest influence on Geoff's progress and it was Ron who decided to convert him to a striker. At that time West Ham was particularly strong in the wing half positions with players like Ronnie Boyce, Eddie Bovington and the young Martin Peters, and Ron felt that Geoff had the physique to be a striker and would get more first team opportunities at the front. But he couldn't have envisaged what was to happen in the next few years. Geoff's career took off like a fairy tale. He got into the England side against West Germany in February 1966 and a few months later he was world famous having become the first – and still the only – man to score a hat trick in a World Cup final.

It had looked as though Jimmy Greaves and Roger Hunt would be the regular striking partnership throughout the finals. But Greaves didn't score in the opening three games and when he was injured the manager, Alf Ramsey, decided to throw in the young and still inexperienced Hurst. He

went into the side for the infamous match against Argentina, scored a goal and kept his place. But it was his three goals against West Germany in the final that earned him worldwide fame and for the rest of that decade I considered him to be one of the finest strikers in the game, certainly the best in England. I recall that shortly after the World Cup, Matt Busby, then manager of Manchester United, made a bid of £200,000 for him – an unheard of fee in those days – but Greenwood replied with a one word telegram, 'No'.

Geoff had all the qualities required of a top class striker – he was strong, brave, worked hard, would run all day and, crucially, could score goals regularly. One of the most memorable features of his game was the ability he had to receive the ball on his chest and shield it. With his back to the goal, he would run to meet a long, high pass, bouncing the ball off his chest to the feet of a team-mate. He was an old fashioned target man who received a great service from players like Bobby Moore and Johnny Byrne. You knocked the ball in to him and he rarely gave it away; he held the ball, led the line superbly and finished clinically. While Jimmy Greaves placed his shots, Geoff powered them in with his cheeks blowing. He scored at roughly the rate of a goal every two games – nearly 200 goals in 400 League matches for West Ham and 24 in 49 England appearances.

His confidence in front of the goal was best illustrated by the purposeful way in which he strode forward to hit penalties with such violence that few goalkeepers had a chance to stop them. I recall one memorable save, though, when Gordon Banks, who had obviously watched Geoff many times training with England, stopped a penalty in a League Cup semi-final at Upton Park. Stoke went on to beat West Ham after four games and then to win the final against Chelsea. Geoff joined Stoke soon afterwards and spent three seasons at the Victoria Ground, still scoring goals. Hurst and Peters perfected the near post goal and it became a West Ham trademark in the 1960s. It was wonderful to watch them playing together with Geoff's strength and running ability carrying him to the near post to meet Martin's perfect crosses. A memorable example of this ploy came in the 1966 World Cup against Argentina when Martin floated a cross to the near post and Geoff flicked in the only goal of the game with his head.

Greenwood thought so highly of Geoff that years later, when he was England manager, he asked his former player to help him in coaching sessions. Geoff was used to demonstrate the type of play that Ron wanted to see from the England strikers. Geoff was then with Telford in the Southern League, but later he moved into management with Chelsea and just missed promotion to Division One. He had a wonderful sporting career and must have been influenced by his father, who had played for Oldham. Geoff was also an accomplished cricketer, playing for Essex in the first class game.

TOMMY HUTCHISON

Tommy Hutchison (winger)
Cardenden 22.9.47
Alloa, Blackpool, Coventry
City, Manchester City,
Burnley, Swansea City
Scotland – 17

In an era when it wasn't easy for wingers to survive, Tommy Hutchison was one who thrived and ensured that old fashioned wing play didn't disappear altogether. Lean and splendidly athletic, he was a player who revelled in the wide open spaces on the flanks and he successfully fought off any moves to turn him into the modern, all-purpose midfield player. Born in Cardenden, Scotland, he was rejected by Blackburn Rovers and Oldham Athletic before Alloa signed him from a team called Dundonald Bluebell and gave him a chance in the Scottish League. Such was the impact he made in his first two seasons that Blackpool, just relegated to Division Two, decided that he was the man to help them win back their place among the élite and they paid £8,000 for him in February 1968.

It was then the fashion to play without wingers; Sir Alf Ramsey had sounded their death knell two years earlier by winning the World Cup

Tommy Hutchison was an old-fashioned winger, but his athletic prowess enabled him to cope with the demands of modern play.

without them. Most wingers had to adapt to new midfield demands, but some, I'm glad to say, survived in their original form – and Tommy was one of them.

I always found him an entertaining player to watch. He was very fast, awesomely fit and it says much for his training that he was still playing for Swansea City in 1987 at the age of 40. Sharp features and a drooping, Mexican-bandit moustache made him a distinctive, easily recognisable figure, but I think most opponents will remember him for his ability to sweep past them and leave them floundering in his wake. He had the skill to take on and beat defenders and the pace to get away from them. Although primarily right footed, he played most of his career on the left wing.

He spent six seasons at Blackpool and, just as they had hoped, helped them to win promotion from Division Two in 1969–70. It was around this time that I first became aware of his talent because he played in the Blackpool side that beat West Ham 4–0 and knocked them out of the FA Cup in the third round in January 1971. In normal circumstances such a defeat wouldn't have been too big a surprise but, what gave this result its infamy was the incident in a Blackpool nightclub on the eve of the match which resulted in four players being fined by the club and Bobby Moore being stripped of the captaincy. That incident was the beginning of the end of Bobby's wonderful career at Upton Park.

Inevitably, Tommy's eye-catching wing play prompted envious glances from many bigger clubs and, when Blackpool were relegated back to Division Two, they decided to capitalise on his talent. They sold him to Coventry in October 1972 for £145,000. It was at Highfield Road that he gained international prominence, winning the first of 17 Scotland caps and playing in the 1974 World Cup finals in West Germany. He spent eight seasons at Coventry which were sadly barren in terms of domestic honours, but when John Bond signed him for Manchester City for £47,000 in October 1980 he very quickly got a taste of the big Wembley occasion.

He was an influential figure in City's FA Cup side that season and played a prominent role in the final against Tottenham. He scored for both sides in a 1–1 draw that went into extra time. He was unlucky when Glenn Hoddle's eighty-first minute free kick flew into the net off his shoulder. The replay of this, the Centenary final, lived up to its billing but, sadly for Hutchison and City, Spurs won a memorable game 3–2. By this time he was 34 and, although he still retained that little bit of Scottish fire which meant that he would never happily accept defeat, the years of teasing the best defences in the First Division were fading rapidly.

In 1982 he went to Hong Kong and played for Bulova for two years and then returned to make a League come-back with Burnley. He played 100 games for Burnley, all 46 League matches in 1984–85 – the year they were relegated to Division Four. That was some achievement for a player approaching his fortieth birthday, and at the end of the season he moved to Swansea and was still playing at the age of 40.

JOHN JACKSON

John Jackson (goalkeeper)
Hammersmith 5.9.42
Crystal Palace, Orient,
Millwall

Some readers may feel that John's inclusion in my 100 greatest is a surprise choice but he had a long and distinguished career in the game and, in my eyes, is well worth a place in any top 100. In a 20-year career he became one of the outstanding exponents of the art of goalkeeping. He was reliable and consistent, although he was scarcely noticed during a career that was spent predominantly with London clubs. He was not a flamboyant goalkeeper but he made an immeasurable contribution at Crystal Palace,

Unsung hero John Jackson was a careful goalkeeper but he was always ready to run the gauntlet of flailing boots when necessary.

Orient and Millwall. A goalkeeper of enduring excellence, he was one of the first to play late into his 30s, making such longevity a fashion among goalkeepers.

If John had joined one of the glamorous First Division clubs I'm sure he would have ended his career with a cabinet full of trophies. As it was, the highlight of his career probably came in the 1968–69 season, when he was ever-present in the Palace side that finished runners-up to Derby in Division Two. He proved to me, as did Don Rogers and Dixie McNeil, that you don't have to play the major part of your career in Division One to be outstandingly good at your profession.

He had good all-round ability but consistency was unquestionably his trademark. He joined Crystal Palace in 1962 on leaving Westminster School, taking over as first choice goalkeeper from Bill Glazier in 1964–65. In the following eight seasons he missed only 12 games. In 1973 he joined Orient and spent six years with them without missing a game, which is a remarkable record. He then went to Millwall and was still playing at nearly 40 years of age. It was at this stage of his career that he collected an unexpected bonus. Bobby Robson's Ipswich team was chasing the UEFA Cup in 1980–81 when they were suddenly hit by a series of injuries to their goalkeepers. Robson asked Jackson if he would like to travel to Widzew Lodz in Poland as goalkeeping cover. He went and wasn't needed but it was his first and only taste of European football.

John was a super chap and playing against him for the first time you could have been forgiven for thinking 'This one doesn't look much like a goalkeeper'. He was a sober character off the field and a very conservative dresser – even his Crystal Palace team-mates used to take the mickey out of him because of his clothes. But he couldn't be faulted when you put him between the posts; he dominated his penalty area, took crosses well and instilled confidence in the defenders around him. He was a cautious and patient goalkeeper who was prepared to plunge in among the flying boots when necessary.

Several top clubs might have been more tempted to buy him had he been a more acrobatic performer who grabbed the headlines. As it was he chose to go about his job quietly and effectively, but few goalkeepers will earn more respect and admiration than John Jackson did during his long career.

LEIGHTON JAMES

Leighton James (winger)
Llwchwyr 16.2.53
Burnley, Derby County,
Queen's Park Rangers,
Swansea City, Sunderland
Wales – 54

Leighton James, a graduate of the very productive youth scheme at Turf Moor, came from the unpronounceable Welsh town of Llwchwyr and was to become one of his country's finest wingers. He could play on both flanks and although primarily right footed he played most of his games on the left wing. He was quite brilliant at times and as well as setting up chances for others he was capable of scoring spectacular goals. The fact that he could cut inside from the left flank and shoot with his right foot was a valuable asset; he could drive the ball, or curl it with equal ease, and the accuracy of his shooting earned him a reputation as a free kick specialist:

A crafty, temperamental player and a spectacular goalscorer, Leighton James would gnaw away at the opposition like toothache.

I played against Leighton many times and have to say that he could be a provocative opponent. He was one of those players who niggled away at you and he was responsible for one of the few cautions of my career. Midway through the second half of a game that West Ham won 5–3 at Turf Moor, Burnley were staging a bit of a revival and Leighton was the man doing the damage with his telling runs down the left side. We caught him with two or three lively tackles to slow him down a bit and it was my misfortune to catch him with the fourth. Tackling not being my strength, I challenged him just as he got his toe to the ball and pushed it into space. I clipped him as he pushed the ball away and he made a meal of the dive; it looked like an awful tackle when in fact it was simply inept. It was one of those situations where the referee felt he had to make an example of one of the West Ham culprits and, unfortunately, it was muggins whose name went in the book.

Leighton gnawed away at the opposition like a toothache and I should think quite a number of players were cautioned for retaliatory tackles made against him. But he was a player of undeniable skill and pace, and was very shrewd and competent, although to look at him off the field you wouldn't have guessed that he was a professional footballer. He wore glasses, had a mild manner and looked more like a university lecturer than a sportsman, but on the field he knew all the tricks. Like many wingers he sometimes felt that he didn't receive the protection he deserved and was usually the first to start complaining to the referee about the opposition.

I think his best years were probably at Burnley where he emerged alongside players like Ralph Coates, Martin Dobson and Dave Thomas. Like them, he was sold for a big fee to help the club balance the books. He spent five years at Turf Moor – scoring 44 goals in 180 games – before Derby signed him for £310,000 in 1975. He spent two seasons at the Baseball Ground and one with Queen's Park Rangers before returning to Burnley in 1978. By this time he was an established Wales international who went on to play a total of 54 games for his country. In 1980 his Wales team-mate John Toshack signed him for Swansea and he was a major influence in helping them to reach the First Division for the first time in the club's history. He finished his playing days with Sunderland.

PAT JENNINGS

Pat Jennings OBE
(goalkeeper)
Newry 12.6.45
Newry Town, Watford,
Tottenham Hotspur, Arsenal
Northern Ireland – 119

Pat Jennings was a prince among goalkeepers. He was probably as reliable, consistent and admired as any goalkeeper I've seen and towards the end of a long and distinguished career he possessed an almost regal air. What struck me about him most as a player, apart from his technical brilliance, was his unflappability and the calming effect he had on those around him. If I were teaching youngsters how to be effective in goal without being flash or elaborate I would choose Pat as my example.

Some goalkeepers excel at one or two aspects of the art, but have a weakness such as not being able to catch crosses or dive at the feet of strikers. In my opinion, though, Pat's game was almost faultless. I thought he was particularly strong at catching crosses and the fact that he was blessed with two of the biggest hands you are likely to see was obviously a bonus. His one handed catch in mid-air became an easily recognised trademark; his timing made it all look so easy and I rarely saw him go for a cross and fail to get it. He either made his move and caught the ball or chose instead to stay on his line. His judgment and reading of situations were superb.

He was also a good shot-stopper and another aspect of goalkeeping that became a Jennings' trademark was his ability to block shots with his feet and legs. It was an unorthodox ploy but a very effective one. He rarely rushed from his goal and committed himself, which is what strikers want goalkeepers to do; he stood up, poised on his toes, waiting for the striker to make the first move. He played until he was 41 and, like John Jackson, he provided a lot of other goalkeepers with the incentive to play on into their late 30s. Even towards the end of his career, when his reflexes were slowing down, he remained among the best 'keepers in the world.

I will always remember his performance for Northern Ireland against England at Wembley when the Irish needed to draw in order to qualify for the 1986 World Cup in Mexico. He was quite outstanding that day and made one remarkable save from Glenn Hoddle, launching himself backwards to save what appeared to be a lost cause and tip the ball from under the bar. Although he wasn't playing full time League football then he had kept himself in excellent shape and played throughout the finals in Mexico. No one could have chosen a more appropriate stage on which to retire. His last international on his forty-first birthday was against Brazil and gave him a record 119 caps.

Pat began life modestly, labouring in a timber yard in Newry and was spotted by Watford while he was playing for the local side. After a year at Vicarage Road he was transferred to Tottenham in 1964 and spent 12 rewarding years at White Hart Lane playing more than 600 games. There were a few gasps of astonishment in North London when Spurs allowed him to move to their rivals Arsenal, a decision Spurs may have regretted when they realised that Pat's career was showing no signs of decline. He won an FA Cup-winners' medal with Spurs in 1967 and made three more Wembley appearances with Arsenal between 1978 and 1980.

I remember playing against him for West Ham in the 1980 FA Cup final at Wembley – how could I forget it? Pat is probably still recovering from the shock of seeing me head a goal past him. He retired after the Mexico World Cup and now devotes much of his time to public relations, charity work and the golf course, where he is a bit of a bandit. He enjoyed an exemplary career but never let the success go to his head; he remained modest and unassuming and I would offer him as an example to all young goalkeepers.

Pat was unquestionably one of the great soccer personalities of the post-war era. He was Ireland's number one for 23 seasons and played a total of 1,098 first class matches.

Pat Jennings – a prince among goalkeepers. He crowned a wonderful career by winning his record 119th cap against Brazil in the 1986 World Cup.

JIMMY JOHNSTONE

Jimmy Johnstone (winger)
Viewpark 30.9.44
Celtic, Sheffield United
Scotland – 23

Jimmy Johnstone was a tiny winger with flaming red hair, an excitable temperament and an original talent. He was, in my opinion, one of the most exciting Scottish players of all time. His best games were on the big occasions and against the most formidable opposition. He was a Lowland Scot, a one-time ball boy with Celtic, who seemed to have a natural affinity with trouble. While the skill of the wee man generated an idolatory matched by few other players in Britain, his off the field behaviour frequently provoked outrage. It was the unpredictable nature of his game that always fascinated me. He had a wonderful ability to take on defenders, wriggle past them and create openings for others. He had an impish, bouncy personality – they called him 'Jinky' at Celtic – and used to have his socks down round his ankles soon after the kick-off, defying defenders to kick him as he delighted the crowds with his teasing dribbles.

If Jimmy's diminutive stature aroused sympathy on the terraces it earned him none from defenders. He was exceptionally talented and brave and was the target for hatchet men around the world. He was a resilient little fellow who would be sent crashing to the ground by a tackle but instantly spring back to his feet. No one who saw the BBC film of the brutal third match between Celtic and Racing Club of Argentina for the World Club championship can forget the fearful punishment meted out to Johnstone. He was eventually sent off in that infamous game – he was just 23 yet it was the fourth dismissal of a short career.

At 5 ft 4 in and $9\frac{1}{2}$ stone, he was, pound for pound, the most explosive and exciting player in Scotland in the 1960s and was probably matched only by Manchester United's George Best in the British Isles. I remember watching him for the first time in 1967 when he played in the Celtic side that became the first British team to win the European Cup. The goals of Tommy Gemmell and Steve Chalmers beat Inter-Milan 2–1 in Lisbon but Johnstone was the player who mesmerised me as I watched the television that night. His jinking runs stretched the famed Italian defence and earned him worldwide recognition. His fan mail came by the bagful from Europe and South America where he became known as 'El Chico'. After that match in Lisbon the late, legendary manager of Celtic, Jock Stein, said of him, 'The wee man put the fear of God in Burgnich. He must have beaten him three or four times in the opening few minutes and it was he who helped win over the local Portuguese in the crowd'.

Stein had a love–hate relationship with Johnstone but, deep down, I suspect he thought of him almost as a son. 'He is not a bad boy, it is just that if there is trouble Jimmy seems to be in the thick of it', Stein said at one time. The Celtic manager twice ordered the suspension of Johnstone by the club – once for arguing with him in the dug out and once for threatening to butt an oponent.

There is no doubt that Jimmy had a self-destructive trait though this

OPPOSITE *The sight that struck fear into the hearts of the world's best defenders. At his peak Jimmy Johnstone was one of the cleverest dribblers in the game.*

136

probably endeared him even more to the Celtic faithful. His most publicised, and best-remembered, misdemeanour came in 1974 when he was with the Scotland squad preparing for a British championship game against England. The Scots were staying at Largs on the coast and, following a few drinks one night, Johnstone ended up alone in a rowing boat with only one oar. He was singing happily, unaware that he was drifting out to sea. Eventually he was rescued by the coastguard and a few days later shrugged off all the fuss and gave a fine display in a 2–0 win over England.

Johnstone reserved his best displays for games against important teams such as Inter-Milan, Red Star Belgrade and Leeds United. He had a morbid fear of flying and in 1968–69 Stein utilised this terror to dramatic effect; he promised Johnstone that he would not be required to travel to Belgrade if Celtic established a four goal lead against Red Star in the second round of the European Cup. Johnstone helped to destroy Red Star in the first leg in Glasgow, scoring twice in a 5–1 victory. He also destroyed Terry Cooper, one of England's greatest full backs, before a record attendance for a European Cup tie of 136,505 the following season. Celtic beat Leeds in the semi-final but lost to Feyenoord in the final in Milan.

Johnstone made his international debut for Scotland against Wales in 1965 and, for all his skill, played only 23 times for his country. His 'wild man' reputation didn't help and he was frequently carpeted by the Scottish Football Association. If he had a weakness as a player it was the one common to so many ball-playing Scots – he was sometimes caught in possession because he refused to hit the simple pass. He tended to over-elaborate but, for me, his entertainment value compensated for most of his shortcomings.

He was a native of Viewpark, Lanarkshire, and was a self-confessed poacher who would spend his spare time roaming the countryside around Glasgow with a shotgun and his Alsatian. His last appearance at Celtic Park was his joint testimonial match with Bobby Lennox in May 1976. Fifty thousand fans watched Celtic beat Manchester United 4–0 and by the end Johnstone had tears in his eyes. As the crowd saluted him, he walked to the terraces and threw them his boots. He later played a handful of games for Sheffield United and San Jose Earthquakes in the United States. He also had a spell on the Celtic coaching staff before joining Highland League side, Elgin City. They sacked him halfway through a two year contract following allegations of eve-of-match drinking sessions.

CLIFF JONES

I was fortunate enough to play a few games against Cliff Jones towards the end of his career and the thing that surprised me about him was his height. He was a bantamweight – not much more than 5 ft 6 in tall – which was curious because having watched him play from the terraces at White Hart Lane the thing that impressed me most was his bravery. For such a little fellow, he had the courage of a lion; I realised that he wasn't tall, but I always assumed that he must have had the strength of a Welsh pit pony.

He was a wiry man and one of his specialities during his great years with Tottenham was the diving header. He would suddenly appear from nowhere and burst through a ruck of defenders to meet a cross with a torpedo like header. It was because of his bravery that the manager at the time, Bill Nicholson, chose Jones to play a vital role in one of the team's free kick routines. Jones would stand on the end of the opposition's defensive

Cliff Jones (winger)
Swansea 7.2.35
Swansea City, Tottenham
Hotspur, Fulham
Wales – 59

Bantamweight Cliff Jones in his first game for Fulham, against Norwich City, after leaving Spurs in 1968. He had the courage of a lion and the strength of a Welsh pit pony.

wall. Danny Blanchflower would chip the free kick over the wall and Jones would peel off and chase after the ball in the hope that he could get it before the goalkeeper did. 'With the ball running away from him over his shoulder and the probability that the goalkeeper would be running at him, it took a brave man to undertake the task', said Nicholson. 'There was no one braver than Jones.'

Cliff came from a famous footballing family in Swansea. His father Ivor was a Welsh international in the 1920s and his uncle Bryn played for Wolves, Arsenal and Wales, and his brother Bryn played for Swansea, Newport, Bournemouth, Northampton and Watford. Cliff began his career with Swansea in 1952 and he spent five years with them before moving to Spurs for £35,000 in 1958, a British record transfer fee for a winger at that time. Soon after moving to White Hart Lane he broke a leg but showed his resilient nature by swiftly recovering from the injury to establish himself as a key figure in the Tottenham League and FA Cup double winning side of 1961.

Although naturally right footed, he played the majority of his games on Tottenham's left flank and in the early 1960s he was recognised as the best left winger in the world. In all, he spent 11 seasons at Tottenham scoring 134 goals in 314 League matches. When you consider that he was essentially a flank player providing crosses for central strikers like Bobby Smith, that goalscoring ratio is quite remarkable and could not be matched by modern wingers. He had a little spring in his step and quite extraordinary pace over a short distance. The speed with which he whipped inside full backs to meet a through ball from John White was a regular feature of Tottenham's attacking play in the early 1960s.

He was an outstanding player for Wales – winning 59 caps – though he is remembered chiefly for his contribution to Tottenham's double year. Sometimes he could be foolishly brave and, because of injuries, missed 13 League games in 1961. Even so, he finished as the club's third highest goalscorer that season. His great years at Tottenham ended in 1968 when he moved to Fulham. He spent just one season at Craven Cottage before retiring.

KEVIN KEEGAN

Kevin couldn't have timed his move from Scunthorpe to Liverpool better because just as he was beginning to make an impact at Anfield in the early 1970s George Best was going off the rails at Manchester United. So the football world was looking for a new superstar and Kevin fitted the bill beautifully. Small, chunky, with infectious good humour, he was a wonderful player, but very different from Best. It was Kevin's ambition, dedication and love of hard work that enabled him to achieve the peak of his potential. His determination to succeed was legendary and something I grew to admire as we became firm friends and room-mates on all of England's trip's abroad. Nothing illustrated this determination more than his battle against a back injury during the 1982 World Cup in Spain.

Kevin had been troubled by pains in his back before the tournament began and I recall one occasion, at the England hotel in Hertfordshire when, having gone down to breakfast leaving him in the bath, I went back to the room 30 minutes later to find him still there, unable to get out because of his back problem. His back troubled him more and more and caused him to miss the first four matches in the World Cup. We were based in Bilbao at the start of the tournament and as days and days of treatment were providing no cure Kevin decided to take matters into his own hands. He knew of a doctor in Hamburg who could manipulate his back into place and he convinced the manager, Ron Greenwood, that he should fly there secretly for treatment. Greenwood agreed in principle, but felt that if Kevin flew from Bilbao it would cause a big stir in the press and that was

Kevin Keegan OBE (striker)
Doncaster 14.2.51
Scunthorpe United, Liverpool,
SV Hamburg, Southampton,
Newcastle United
England — 63

Sometimes this was the only way to stop Kevin Keegan, an inspirational England captain whose determination and persistence made him difficult to knock off the ball.

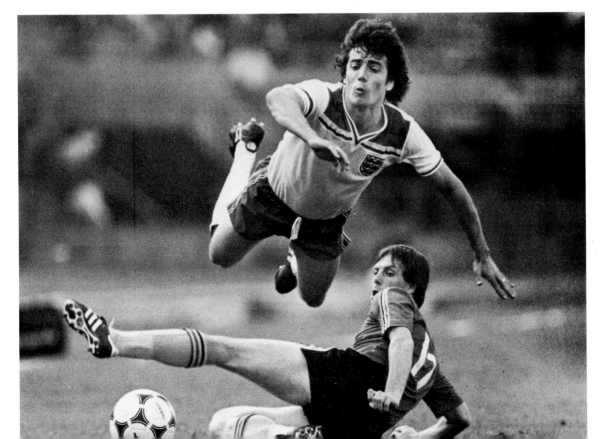

something he wanted to avoid. It was decided that Kevin should catch an early morning flight from Madrid, so late one night he slipped unnoticed from the team hotel and drove overnight to the Spanish capital. He returned two days later feeling much better and, as a result of the treatment that he received in Hamburg, was able to play for 25 minutes as a substitute in our final World Cup game against Spain.

We came on together as substitutes in that match and very nearly secured the win that we needed to reach the semi-finals. For many years people had made a lot of the telepathic understanding that was supposed to exist between us, but there was no such thing. It was simply that as a midfield player I would get the ball and look up for a target and Kevin's appetite for the game meant that he was always moving into space and was invariably the easiest player to find with a pass. He was short for a striker, stocky, strong and hard to knock off the ball — in fact, physically similar to Maradona. Kevin was an excellent finisher with good anticipation and acceleration, and he was powerful in the air for someone of his height. In tight situations he could shield the ball well and twist out of trouble. His goalscoring talent developed at Liverpool where he established a great relationship with John Toshack, feeding off the knock-downs from the big Wales striker. By the time he ran Bertie Vogts ragged in the 1977 European Cup final he was one of the world's great players.

The three years that Keegan spent with Hamburg enhanced his game further, teaching him in particular how to overcome man-to-man marking, and his status in the game was acknowledged when he won the European Footballer of the Year title in consecutive seasons. His years abroad inevitably broadened his character. He was a comedian and motivator in the dressing room and a good captain who always conducted himself as befits a top sporting personality. Kevin was a great example to youngsters just like Bobby Charlton had been years before.

Kevin was a terrible fidget during his playing career; he could never sit and read a book. He always had to be doing something. I'm quite surprised how well he's adapted to his new way of life in Spain, where he sits in the sunshine or works at improving his golf and tennis. He didn't play again for England after the 1982 World Cup, which I think was a shame. The new manager, Bobby Robson, decided to leave him out of the squad when, for me, he was at 31 still the best striker in England. There was no justification for leaving him out — as he proved with two good years at Newcastle.

Even when Kevin retired he could have gone on, but he felt he had lost a yard of pace. The fixture that convinced him that it was over was an FA Cup tie against his old club, Liverpool, at Anfield. Newcastle lost 4–0 and there were occasions in that game when he simply couldn't match the pace of Mark Lawrenson, who was marking him. He knew what he wanted to do but didn't have the physical prowess to do it. Kevin was a perfectionist; he didn't want to be second best and that game, more than any other, made him realise that it was time to go.

HOWARD KENDALL

I remember Howard particularly well as a young player and I'm sure that many people with West Ham affiliations would say the same. That is, quite simply, because Howard was Preston's surprise choice in their FA Cup final side against West Ham at Wembley. Howard was a brilliant youngster who played against West Ham just 20 days before his eighteenth birthday. At that time he was the youngest player to appear in the FA Cup final – a distinction that he held until West Ham's Paul Allen played in the 1980

Howard Kendall (midfield)
Ryton-on-Tyne 22.5.46
Preston North End, Everton,
Birmingham City, Stoke City,
Blackburn Rovers

Even as an outstanding midfield player, Howard Kendall showed an aptitude for organising the team – a strength that was to stand him in good stead as a manager.

final against Arsenal. In 1964 I was soon to become an apprentice at West Ham and I wasn't of sufficient status to warrant a ticket to Wembley, but I remember watching the game on television. Preston were the underdogs from the Second Division but they gave West Ham a close game before losing 3–2. I took a particular interest in Howard because he was only a couple of years older than me and all the pre-match build up had been focused on him.

Howard was a wing half from the old school whose attitude and consistency were very similar to John Hollins'. He was a steady passer who defended well, made good forward runs but didn't score many goals. He collected Football League representative honours and Under–23 caps and was unlucky not to get into the senior side. He was good enough to have played for England and, at times during his career with Everton, his influence in midfield was awesome. It was at Everton that he enjoyed his greatest success, playing on the right side of that wonderful midfield trio of Kendall, Ball and Harvey which provided the cornerstone of Everton's championship victory in 1970.

I always admired Howard's organisational ability on the field and it was no surprise to me when Everton appointed him manager. He had his problems in the early days of his managerial reign, but eventually got it right, steering Everton to championship wins again in 1985 and 1987. Significantly, Everton's re-emergence from Liverpool's shadow coincided with the appointment of Howard's old playing colleague Colin Harvey as first team coach at Goodison Park. They had worked together successfully as players and they enjoyed a new lease of life in management. The partnership eventually came to an end after their League championship win in 1987. Howard felt that he had achieved all he could at Goodison Park and the dual attraction of European football and a king's ransom for a salary enticed him to Athletic Bilbao in Spain.

DENIS LAW

Denis was one of the great strikers and characters in the modern game. He had grace, flair and magnetism and, of course, played for Manchester United when they were probably the most glamorous team in Europe. He was a skinny, pale, young Scot with glasses when the legendary Bill Shankly first signed him for Huddersfield in 1957, but he developed into one of the most dangerous and athletic strikers of the 1960s. He spent three years at Huddersfield before Manchester City signed him. He spent one season at Maine Road, scoring 21 goals in 44 League games and attracting the attention of Torino. The Italian club paid £100,000 for him in June 1961.

By this time he had already shown an astonishing instinct in front of the goal and in one FA Cup tie against Luton Town scored six times. Unfortunately, the match was abandoned and Luton won the replayed game. He had only one season in Italy and returned to Manchester with United in 1962. It was at Old Trafford, alongside players like Bobby Charlton and George Best, that he enjoyed his most magical years, winning two League titles and an FA Cup-winners' medal against Leicester in 1963.

Denis Law (striker)
Aberdeen 24.2.40
Huddersfield Town,
Manchester City, Torino,
Manchester United
Scotland — 55

The predatory Denis Law, sleeves tucked into his fists, finished most of his goal chances with deadly efficiency.

He was a brave, wiry, determined striker with terrific reflexes, blistering pace and the ability to out-jump taller defenders. He liked to play with his shirt hanging loose over his shorts and the shirt cuffs bunched in his fists. His blond hair and the one arm raised to salute a goal helped establish the Law legend. His ability to snap up half chances in the turmoil of the penalty area and score with spectacular overhead kicks made him one of the game's most exciting strikers in one of the game's most attractive teams.

The transition to the international stage frequently brought the best out of Denis and in 55 games for Scotland he scored 30 goals. Nothing motivated him quite as powerfully as the England–Scotland clashes and on the day that the rest of the footballing fraternity was watching England's 1966 World Cup triumph he was playing golf and on hearing the result is supposed to have said; 'That's really spoiled my day'. But the biggest disappointment of his career must have been missing Manchester United's 1968 European Cup final triumph over Benfica because of injury.

In 10 years at Old Trafford he scored 171 goals in 300 League games and in 1973 returned to Manchester City for one last season in an illustrious career. He scored nine goals in his final 22 games with City and one of them was laced with bitter irony. With a typical, cheeky piece of improvisation, he backheeled the goal in the local derby with United that sent his old team down into the Second Division. There was no arm raised in triumph on that occasion. Of all the goals he scored that was the one that gave him the least pleasure.

FRANCIS LEE

'Franny' was a bustling, sturdy little striker who was a key member of the very exciting Manchester City forward line in the team built by Joe Mercer and Malcolm Allison. He had a barrel chest and was slightly portly in appearance but was one of the most effective strikers of the 1960s and 1970s. He began his career at Bolton Wanderers in 1960 and scored 90 goals in 200 League games for them before moving into the big time with City in 1967. He played alongside some great attacking names like Mike Summerbee, Colin Bell and, later, Rodney Marsh.

Francis Lee (striker)
West Houghton 29.4.44
Bolton Wanderers, Manchester City, Derby County
England — 27

It was impossible to intimidate Manchester City's Franny Lee, a tenacious, barrel-chested striker and a prolific goalscorer.

He had started his career as a winger but by the time he went to City he was playing a more orthodox striking role. He was one of the most aggressive forwards I can remember and had a ruthless streak that meant he could be a formidable opponent. He tended to irritate his markers and, inevitably, was often the victim of heavy challenges. He won a lot of penalties for City — and wasn't really too fussy about how he won them. There was a period during City's most successful spell in the early 1970s when the fact that they were awarded so many penalties became a topical talking point. Many of them were awarded for fouls against Franny and he converted most with ease. In 1971–72 he scored 13 penalties which was a record at the time.

In six years with City he scored 112 goals in 250 League matches and was a figure of immense influence in a four year spell in the early 1970s when City won the League title, the FA Cup, the League Cup and the European Cup-winners' Cup. He was also a vital part of Sir Alf Ramsey's England squad and had gone to Mexico to defend the World Cup in 1970. He scored 10 goals in 27 appearances for England.

I always enjoyed watching him, because he was a bouncy type of player who took a lot of knocks but was never downhearted. It was impossible to intimidate him; in fact, the more aggressive the marking the more he appeared to enjoy it. He left City in 1974 and joined Derby County whom he helped to win the League title in 1975. He scored 25 goals in 60 games for Derby before retiring to concentrate on a highly successful paper business that eventually secured him millionaire status.

GARY LINEKER

I can remember Leicester City putting four goals past West Ham once and the lad who caught my eye that day was Gary Lineker. I asked about him after the match, thinking his name might be worth a mention to the England manager, and I was told that he was Scottish! He was, of course, born in Leicester and was destined to become one of the most prolific England marksmen of the 1980s. The thing that impressed me about him, then and now, was his lightning speed and his astute reading of the game. There have been many quick strikers in the game but what gives Lineker the edge is the fact that he knows when best to utilise his speed. The timing of his runs is excellent, the positions he takes invariably provide scoring opportunities, and so long as the service to him is good enough he is a very difficult opponent to stop. He has the natural speed to carry him into scoring positions and to that he has added the composure that is necessary in front of the goal. He has become an outstanding finisher, able to score with both feet or his head.

He made his international debut for England as a substitute against Scotland in 1984 and two years later he established himself as a striker of the highest quality when he scored six goals and finished as the leading marksman in the 1986 World Cup. He scored a hat trick against Poland in Monterrey to pull England back from the brink of a shameful World Cup exit. They were the first goals that England scored in Mexico and they restored the reputation of Bobby Robson's men. They also provided the first signs of a blossoming partnership between Gary and the Liverpool (formerly Newcastle) striker, Peter Beardsley. Lineker's three goals in the Estadio Universitario illustrated all his strengths. On a warm evening, in the shadow of Monterrey's saddleback mountain, he outpaced defenders to slide in a right wing cross from Everton team-mate Gary Stevens after just seven minutes. The Poles, forced to emerge from their defensive stronghold gave Lineker even more scope. He volleyed home a cross from Steve Hodge on the left and had the speed and wit to capitalise on a mistake by the Polish goalkeeper.

In my opinion Gary has one area of his game that he needs to improve if he wants to be acknowledged as a complete, all-round striker and I'm sure that his first manager at Barcelona, Terry Venables, stressed the point. He needs to work on his ability to dribble with the ball and to create his own chances because there is no doubt that he is a striker who relies on a good and consistent service from team-mates. If that service isn't forthcoming his contribution to the game is limited.

After the seven years at Leicester, Gary moved to Everton, but his success in the World Cup put him on the international market and was to change his life. Only weeks after returning from Mexico and after just one season at Everton they reluctantly accepted Barcelona's huge bid of £2.75 million for him. It was a deal that should go a long way towards making

Gary Lineker (striker)
Leicester 30.11.60
Leicester City, Everton,
Barcelona
England – 35

him financially secure for life. He's a warm, amiable lad who conducts himself in an exemplary fashion on and off the field. He is completely unspoiled by his success and I'm sure he will continue to be an excellent ambassador for the English game.

His goalscoring reputation ensured that he was the most feared striker in the European Championships in West Germany in June 1988. He scored in the warm-up games against Colombia and Switzerland, taking his total of England goals to 26 in 28 starts. By any standards he is a quite remarkable striker and, if he can maintain his scoring rate, he seems certain to beat Bobby Charlton's all-time record of 49 goals for England.

Gary Lineker scores against Holland at Wembley in Spring 1988, but I'm sure he would have preferred to have saved the goal for the decisive European Championship tie that summer — a match the Dutch won 3–1.

NAT LOFTHOUSE

Nat Lofthouse was a bludgeoning, old-fashioned type of centre forward and one of the biggest names in football when I was a youngster in the 1950s. The son of a Bolton coalman, he spent the war years at the pit face and when he finally established himself in the Bolton Wanderers team in 1946, the broad shoulders, deep chest and raw courage gave him a physical presence that was soon to be feared throughout Europe.

He had attended the same school as the legendary Tommy Lawton whom he was eventually to replace in the England side. He didn't have the skill of Lawton, but he made up for that with his battering-ram strength. He was a remorseless pursuer of lost causes. He was an awesome header of the ball and he epitomised the typical English centre forward of the 1950s. Ron Greenwood remembers Lofthouse well in those far off days. 'As a centre half, I grew to appreciate what it meant to play against Nat', he recalls. 'He used to make towering leaps at the far post and head the ball with tremendous power. He had mobility and a good touch and was very difficult to play against.'

He was almost as prolific a goalscorer as Jimmy Greaves; he scored 30 goals in 33 appearances for England and 285 goals in 505 games for Bolton – his only club in a 15-year playing career. He scored on his debut for England against Yugoslavia in 1951 and was still banging them in when he was recalled to the side against the USSR in 1959. He was 35 then but still got on the score sheet in a 5–0 victory.

But his most famous game for England came in Vienna's giant Prater Stadium in 1952. Austria were one of the most accomplished sides in Europe and were holding England to a 2–2 draw when the game suddenly turned sour. Austria were the intimidators, but no one intimidated Lofthouse. Nine minutes from the end he collected a pass from Tom Finney and began a surging run that took him from the halfway line to the Austrian penalty area. As the Austrian goalkeeper charged out at him, Lofthouse didn't falter or shorten his step. He hit the ball cleanly into the corner of the net and, such was the impact when he and the goalkeeper collided, that Nat had to leave the field for treatment. For his efforts that day – he scored two goals – he was christened 'The Lion of Vienna' by the popular press – a name that stuck with him until he retired. The following year he was in the headlines again scoring in every round of the FA Cup, including the final. Although Blackpool, and Stanley Mattews, won 4–3 at Wembley, Lofthouse had the consolation that season of being voted Footballer of the Year.

His aggression and unflinching challenges gnawed at the most efficient defences and exposed any weakness in character. And, although an affable man off the field, there were times when his strength was coarsely employed. His only other FA Cup final appearance came towards the end of his career in 1958 when Bolton faced Manchester United just three months after the Munich air disaster. United, quite naturally, had the sympathy of the nation,

Nat Lofthouse (striker)
Bolton 27.8.25
Bolton Wanderers
England – 33

but Bolton won the Cup 2–0, both goals coming from – yes, you've guessed it – Nat Lofthouse. The second goal provoked protests from United, howls from the Wembley crowd and is still debated to this day. Harry Gregg, the United goalkeeper, stretching to catch a high ball, was hit by the bear-like Lofthouse with a shoulder charge that carried both goalkeeper and ball into the net. Gregg was hurt and had to leave the field, but the goal stood. That incident, which would not be tolerated today, played a major role in winning greater protection for goalkeepers.

A triumphant Nat Lofthouse with the FA Cup after Bolton Wanderers' 2–0 victory over Manchester United in 1958. Lofthouse scored both goals, perfect examples of his aggressive, no-nonsense style of play.

MALCOLM MACDONALD

With long, shaggy sideburns, bandy legs and fist raised in triumph, Malcolm Macdonald became a cult figure at Newcastle. They have invariably established a special rapport with their strikers at St James' Park and for the terrace faithful at Newcastle no striker was quite as special as 'Supermac'. He had explosive pace and a ferocious left foot shot. In full flight he was a thrilling spectacle and I would estimate that 90 per cent of his goals were thudding left foot drives that brought the fans jumping from their seats in delight.

Malcolm began his career as a modest full back with Tonbridge and although Fulham signed him in 1968 and converted him into a centre forward it wasn't until he moved to Luton a year later that his goalscoring potential really became apparent. Under the shrewd guidance of manager Harry Haslam, he enjoyed sensational form at Kenilworth Road, scoring 49 goals in 88 matches. Inevitably they were forced by the economics of football to sell him and Newcastle paid a club record £185,000 in 1971. The crowd loved him from the very start and he repaid them in full, scoring 95 goals in 187 games. I think Malcolm had a lot to thank the midfield player, Terry Hibbitt, for during his five years at St James' Park. It was Hibbitt who provided the service – the long through pass – and Macdonald thrived on it, regularly outpacing defenders before unleashing a waist high drive from around 20 yards.

He played in the Newcastle side which was beaten 3–0 by Liverpool in the 1974 FA Cup final and by 1976, when he was an established member of the England squad, he was looking for fresh challenges on the domestic front. Arsenal stepped in with a £330,000 bid and signed him and, to Malcolm's credit, he maintained his scoring rate of a goal every two games. He was a prolific goalscorer, but not a great team player; he was a striker who relied heavily on a good service. Unfortunately for him he couldn't take his goalscoring form onto the international stage. He played on 14 occasions for England, but scored in only one of those games – against Cyprus at Wembley in April 1975 – and typically he got five goals.

Built like a toy bull, he liked the ball over the defence so that he could charge after it, bulldozing his way through challenging defenders. But playing on the international stage, frequently against the foreign sweeper system, it's necessary for a striker to be comfortable receiving the ball at his feet and I think that's where Malcolm found the transition to international football difficult. Sadly, his career was curtailed at 29 after three years with Arsenal. He had problems with his knees and once he lost the explosive running that allowed him to burst past defenders his game inevitably suffered. But, in a short League career of just 269 games, he scored a total of 191 goals which is a phenomenal ratio by modern standards.

I think that retirement came hard for Malcolm. There were still many challenges in the game for him when he was forced to hang up his boots.

Malcolm Macdonald (striker)
Fulham 7.1.50
Fulham, Luton Town,
Newcastle United, Arsenal
England – 14

He was a confident player, bordering on arrogant, and there's no doubt that he enjoyed the spotlight and the creation of the Macdonald legend. Management tempted him and he tried it with Fulham, where he had begun his League career as a player. He later went into the pub business but re-emerged in football as one of the agents involved in the transfer of the first Brazilian to English football – Mirandinha, who joined Malcolm's old club, Newcastle. Shortly after negotiating that deal in 1987 he went back into management with Huddersfield, although his tenancy there was short-lived. The club languished at the bottom of Division Two on his arrival; he was unable to reverse the trend and was sacked at the end of the season.

The toothless grin of Malcolm Macdonald became a familiar sight at St James's Park, where his 95 goals earned him the acclaim of the Geordie faithful.

ROY McFARLAND

When Roy was partnering Colin Todd in the Derby side in the 1970s I think they formed as good a centre back partnership as I ever played against in League football. Of the two, Roy was the more complete player and, but for injury, would have had a much longer international career with England. He was a complete, all-round centre half and I was always amazed by his prodigious heading ability because he was only 5 ft 11 in tall. He was a very dominant figure in the air.

Whenever West Ham played against Derby I would always try to bend my crosses away from Roy because he was very mobile and good on his feet and if the ball was in the air anywhere near him you could be sure that he would get to it. He was quick for a defender, a sharp tackler and he

Roy McFarland (centre back)
Liverpool 5.4.48
Tranmere Rovers, Derby County, Bradford City
England – 28

Roy McFarland, one of the most astute centre halves since the war. His international career came to a brutal end when his Achilles' tendon snapped at Wembley.

timed his tackles to perfection. He read the game well, passed well and rarely lost the cool confidence that seemed to accompany whatever he did on the pitch; he was pretty good at everything.

Roy was born in Liverpool and spent just over one season with Tranmere Rovers before Brian Clough decided that he was the defender to help Derby out of Division Two. He did just that. He played in all 42 games and scored nine goals as Derby won the Second Division title in 1969. He then helped Derby to win the First Division title in 1972 and again in 1975.

He was a polished, classic centre half who had a good footballing brain and it didn't take Sir Alf Ramsey long to recognise his qualities. Roy made his England debut in Malta in 1971 and would have made far more than 28 international appearances had it not been for an Achilles' tendon injury which he received playing for England. He climbed for a high ball, landed awkwardly on the pitch and lay there shouting. The physiotherapist came onto the pitch and immediately called for the doctor who told us not to touch his leg. The Achilles' tendon had snapped and you could see it twitching in Roy's leg.

It was a great shame because that injury brought his international career to an early end although he continued to play for Derby and after 14 seasons at the Baseball Ground moved on to Bradford City. As player–manager he led them out of the Fourth Division in 1981–82 but soon after that triumph he was tempted back to the Baseball Ground as assistant to Peter Taylor. He still played the occasional game and when Taylor left in April 1984 Roy was briefly put in charge until the appointment of Arthur Cox. Cox persuaded Roy to stay on as his assistant and together they guided Derby to the Second Division championship in 1987.

DANNY McGRAIN

Danny McGrain is one of the Celtic legends. In the mid-1970s many claimed that he was probably the world's finest attacking full back, which was an accolade he bore modestly. He was a player of extraordinary courage and will power, overcoming diabetes and a fractured skull to establish himself as one of the all-time greats of Scottish football. As a youngster on one of those sprawling Scottish housing estates, McGrain was a Glasgow Rangers fan, like most of his family. Rangers watched him and were very impressed, but when he told them his name, Daniel Fergus McGrain, they immediately assumed that the boy was a Catholic. Religious bigotry being what it was – and to a certain degree still is – in Glasgow, Rangers declined to sign him. It was a blunder, of course; McGrain was a Protestant and when Celtic watched him they had no hesitation in signing him.

That was in 1967 when Celtic were the European Cup holders and one of the most respected teams in the world. Danny had the good fortune to learn the basics of the game in the Celtic reserve side that included other outstanding youngsters like Kenny Dalglish, Lou Macari, George Connelly and David Hay. Such was the obvious promise of the Parkhead nursery team that the players became known as the 'Quality Street Kids'. Unlike the others, McGrain effectively spent his entire career with Celtic. He became club captain, made more than 600 first team appearances and remains Celtic's most honoured player at international level. Although his former team-mate Dalglish played more times for Scotland, all McGrain's 62 appearances came while he was on the Celtic staff.

At first he was considered a midfield player but Celtic's legendary manager, Jock Stein, persuaded him that his best position was right back. It was here that he made his first team debut in a Scottish League Cup match against Dundee United in August 1970. As a right back he was encouraged to express his natural bent for overlapping along the wing and I always felt that his attacking play was his greatest strength. Although he created lots of problems with his dashing runs, this inclination to go forward sometimes rebounded leaving space at the back for a good winger to exploit. He was lean, fit, quick and sharp in the tackle and had hard, craggy features that reflected his resilient character. He must have had deep reserves of determination because he experienced traumas that would have ended the careers of most professional footballers. The first came in 1972 when he suffered a fractured skull as a result of a clash of heads. He was out of action for six months but came back with renewed confidence to win a place in the Scotland side against Wales the following year and so began a nine-year spell in the national team.

Although Danny was more accustomed to playing on the right, Scotland often played him at left back in his early appearances to accommodate the talented Sandy Jardine of Rangers. But, no matter where McGrain played, his pace and composure were combined with a natural competitive edge to

Danny McGrain MBE (full back)
Glasgow 1.5.50
Celtic, Hamilton Academicals
Scotland – 62

make him one of the world's most accomplished defensive players. He missed Scotland's disastrous 1978 World Cup because of a serious ankle injury but it was the discovery that he had contracted diabetes, and his subsequent fight to overcome the disease, that best illustrated his remarkable determination. He played through the group matches in the 1974 World Cup in West Germany with a raging thirst. He was losing weight rapidly but it wasn't until he returned home that diabetes was diagnosed. He was told that had he played in one more match without treatment he could have slipped into a fatal coma.

Showing typical courage and maturity, he faced up squarely to the condition as a permanent one. Daily insulin injections and a careful diet enabled him to continue as a professional athlete. Celtic initially decided to keep the illness a secret, but McGrain later made his condition public in the hope that his experiences would be of some benefit to other sufferers.

At the end of season 1986–87 Celtic gave McGrain a free transfer. During his years with the club they won the Scottish title nine times and the Scottish Cup seven times. He had a brief spell with Hamilton but for Danny McGrain, the fighter, the great years were over.

Scotland v England, 1982. Danny McGrain, an accomplished tackler, looks for the right attacking option before committing himself.

JIMMY McILROY

As a schoolboy playing an inside forward role I used to watch all the great players in my position hoping to pick up a few tips and Jimmy McIlroy was one of those I grew to admire very much indeed. I enjoyed watching him chiefly because of his close control when in possession of the ball and the accuracy of his long passing. He was the sort of player who stamped his personality on a game and whenever I saw Burnley play he was invariably the the man who caught the eye. Ron Greenwood was also an admirer of the McIlroy style. He remembers him as a cool, measured performer; 'Like all great players he always seemed to have time on the ball', Ron told me. 'He was a natural player who was rarely caught in possession. His great strength was the consistency of his service to the centre forward and, largely because of that, he became the architect of the great Burnley side of the late 1950s and early 1960s.'

Jimmy spent 12 years at Turf Moor, but made his name initially as an inside forward of immense promise with Glentoran in Northern Ireland. In March 1953 Burnley paid £7,000 for him, which even in those days was a bargain transfer fee. His authority in midfield and long, probing forward passes became one of the key features of Burnley's play in the 1950s. Two years after joining Burnley the Northern Ireland selectors recognised his ability by selecting him for the first time to make his international debut against England. By the time he was selected to play for Great Britain against the Rest of Europe in 1955 he had become a regular in the Irish side where he seemed to enjoy an almost telepathic understanding with the Tottenham captain Danny Blanchflower. He and Blanchflower were two of the finest midfield players in the world at that time, and later in the 1950s I can remember watching these two greats of the game testing each other in First Division battles at White Hart Lane.

McIlroy's influence played a major role in Burnley's championship triumph of 1960 but, the following year, it was the turn of Blanchflower's Tottenham to dominate the game. They became the first team this century to win the fabled League and FA Cup double. Tottenham were probably the more accomplished team, with Burnley the most serious threat to their domination, and when the two sides met in the 1962 FA Cup final at Wembley the match was billed, quite naturally, as the 'Clash of the Giants'. Burnley had a super team with players like Adam Blacklaw, Jimmy Adamson, John Connelly and Ray Pointer but it was the calm and poise of McIlroy that most impressed me. Spurs, playing in their second consecutive FA Cup final, won 3–1.

In March 1963, after nearly 500 games and more than 100 goals, McIlroy moved to Stoke City for £25,000. When he left Burnley they were one of the top clubs in the country and his reputation must have helped them to attract many of the good young players who were later to become the life-blood of the club and give them one of the most productive youth schemes

Jimmy McIlroy (midfield)
Lambeg 25.10.31
Glentoran, Burnley, Stoke City, Oldham Athletic
Northern Ireland – 55

Cool performer Jimmy McIlroy. 'He was a natural player who was rarely caught in possession.'

in the country. He was 32 when he moved to Stoke and far from finished. He made an immediate impression, helping them to clinch the Second Division title in 1962–63. He also played a further handful of games for the Irish side, taking his total to 55 caps, which included all Northern Ireland's games in the 1958 World Cup in Sweden. The fact that he scored 10 goals for Ireland – only Gerry Armstrong has scored more since the war – has assured him of a place in the folklore of Irish soccer. He played 100 games for Stoke before moving to Oldham for a brief spell and he retired in 1967.

Billy Wright
All-Sport

ABOVE: *Alan Hansen*
All-Sport/David Cannon

FAR RIGHT: *Bobby Moore*
Colorsport

RIGHT: *Ian Rush*
All-Sport/David Cannon

ABOVE: *Jimmy Greaves*
All-Sport

RIGHT: *Jack Charlton (left) and
Frank McLintock* Colorsport

Dave Mackay (left) and George
Best   Bob Thomas

ABOVE: *Malcolm Macdonald*
All-Sport

RIGHT: *Bobby Charlton*
Bob Thomas

Glenn Hoddle
All-Sport/David Cannon

Gary Lineker   All-Sport

DAVE MACKAY

Dave Mackay and Danny Blanchflower provided the heart of a Spurs side that was one of the best I've seen in the game. They complemented each other perfectly, Dave providing the guts and Danny the guile. Dave joined Tottenham from Hearts and the man who signed him, Bill Nicholson, has often said that the capture of Mackay was his best day's work. Dave was the strong, big-hearted, tough-tackling dynamo that every successful side needs. I used to go along to White Hart Lane to watch Spurs as a youngster and one of the most impressive sights in those days was the power and purpose of Mackay's sliding tackles. They often seemed to begin about 10 feet from the opponent, but he ploughed into attackers with great bravery, usually taking the ball cleanly, but occasionally taking the man, too.

Dave's competitive spirit helped him attain a quite remarkable collection of medals. He was already a Scotland Schoolboy international when he joined Heart of Midlothian from Newtongrange Star as a 17-year-old in 1952. Playing in the same side as Alex Young, he won winners' medals in the Scottish League, League Cup (twice) and FA Cup and played in the Scotland team in the 1958 World Cup in Sweden. But there was a price to pay for his lion-hearted bravery. In December 1963, when playing for Spurs against Manchester United in a European Cup-winners' Cup tie at Old Trafford, a collision with Noel Cantwell resulted in a broken leg.

Although not that tall, he was a strong, physical player and his barrel-chest gave him an intimidating appearance. He was a determined Scot who didn't know the meaning of the word defeat. Billy Bonds, my 'minder' for many years at West Ham, reminds me a lot of Dave Mackay. In a sense, Dave enjoyed three careers; he won the first of 22 Scottish caps with Hearts in 1957 then he moved to Spurs where he played in the League and FA Cup double winning team of 1961. He collected two further FA Cup-winners' medals and was in the side that reached the European Cup-winners' Cup final in 1963 although he didn't play in the destruction of Atletico Madrid in Rotterdam.

He had 10 great years at White Hart Lane before moving to Derby County, whose manager Brian Clough saw in Mackay the inspiration which would steer his club to Division One. He was one of the players who provided the foundation for Clough's championship winning team. By then he was in the back four but the aggression was undiluted. He had recovered from two broken legs – the second of which he suffered as he was recovering from the first accident. He knew only one way to play, and that was hard; there was no way he could ease his way back. The injuries threatened his career but he showed enormous character in the way he fought back to play again.

He wasn't just a ball winner. Predominantly left footed, he was also a good distributor of the ball and I can remember him combining his tackling and passing to devastating effect in one match against Manchester United

Dave Mackay (midfield)
Edinburgh 14.11.34
Heart of Midlothian,
Tottenham Hotspur, Derby
County, Swindon Town
Scotland – 22

in the mid-1960s. The big games between the top of the League teams were among the highlights of the season and were always thunderous occasions – the sort of matches that brought the best out of Dave. By 1971 a long, hard career was beginning to take its toll and he moved from Derby to Swindon where he became player-manager. Eighteen months later he became manager of Nottingham Forest and, after less than a year, moved back to Derby, succeeding Clough and adding further honours to a distinguished career winning the First Division championship in 1975. In 1977 he became Walsall manager but the following year moved to the Middle East where he won the Kuwaiti championship five times.

After nine years in the Middle East he demonstrated his enduring love of the game by returning to Britain to become manager of Doncaster Rovers, in Division Three. He was immediately joined by Joe Kinnear, a former team-mate at Spurs, who followed him from Kuwait. He is one of the few men to have won the League title both as player and manager. Remembered as a folk hero at both Tottenham and Derby, his was a career rich in achievement.

Signed for Derby by Brian Clough, Dave Mackay, in turn, succeeded Clough as manager and led his club to the First Division title.

FRANK McLINTOCK

Frank will always be remembered as the inspirational captain of the Arsenal side that won the League and FA Cup double in 1971. But that was just one of many highlights in a career that spanned almost 20 years and began with Shawfield Juniors in Glasgow. Leicester City signed him in 1957 and after two or three seasons learning the business in the reserves he won a first team place and never looked back. In those days he was a midfield player and in five years at Filbert Street he made his international debut for Scotland and played in two FA Cup finals. He was in the Leicester teams, with the great Gordon Banks, that lost the 1961 FA Cup final to Spurs and the 1963 final to Manchester United.

In 1964 Arsenal signed him and a career that was already making good progress really began to take off. He formed an impressive centre back partnership with one of Highbury's unsung heroes, Peter Simpson, and although neither was particularly tall or especially quick they were rarely exposed. Frank was an excellent reader of the game. His timing and spring made him a dominant figure in the air and Arsenal used his power to good effect at corner kicks and free kicks. He was a very consistent performer and eventually an inspiring and tactically astute captain. He was an influential figure in Arsenal's eclipse of the fabled double in 1971 and, not surprisingly, he was voted Footballer of the Year that season.

He was typical of many Scottish defenders – a determined battler who never gave up until the last kick. He epitomised the spirit of the 1971 double team, which was not the most gracious or entertaining of sides but had tremendous qualities in terms of discipline, character and organisation; McLintock was the man who ensured that the machine worked to its full capacity every Saturday afternoon. You would frequently see him in the dying minutes of matches that season charging forward to get his head to a corner kick and then racing back to recover his defensive position before the opposition broke away. He was one of the great captains of that era and it has always surprised me that he won only nine Scottish caps between 1963 and 1971. He deserved more in my opinion.

In 1973 he moved to QPR where he formed another outstanding defensive partnership with David Webb. They provided the experience in a colourful and exciting Rangers side under the management of Dave Sexton. McLintock was once again a figure of immense influence and was instrumental in helping the club to its highest ever position – second in Division One, just one point behind Liverpool in 1976. That side hardly dropped a point in the run-in to the end of the season and it was typical of McLintock that he was battling to overtake Liverpool until the last kick of the season. Since retiring he has worked in management and coaching with Leicester City, Brentford and Millwall and has also been in demand as a match analyst by the television and radio stations.

There is no doubt in my mind that his ability as a coach played a

Frank McLintock MBE (centre back)
Glasgow 28.12.39
Leicester City, Arsenal, Queen's Park Rangers
Scotland – 9

significant role in helping John Docherty's Millwall team to win the Second Division championship in 1988 and to climb into Division One for the first time in the club's 103-year history.

An outstanding centre back, Frank McLintock was probably the most influential figure in Arsenal's fabled League and FA Cup double of 1971.

RODNEY MARSH

I had no hesitation about including Rodney among my top 100 players because he was such an exciting and entertaining personality. He was a bit of a Bohemian and whenever I saw him he was invariably wearing a tee-shirt, jeans and flip flops and looked as though he had just come off the beach. He liked to be different and I think that's what made him one of the most colourful players of the 1960s and 1970s. He wasn't just an entertainer, either. His great days were with QPR and Manchester City and it says something for his reputation that when we played either of those sides his was the first name mentioned in the team-talks; he was a player we ignored at our peril.

You could never be sure how he would perform on the day but you couldn't afford to take a chance with him. When he was on song he could be devastating. His close control and his dribbling ability in tight situations were wonderful to watch. He loved to make defenders look vulnerable and foolish and by playing to the crowd he became quite a folk hero. He was a two footed player who could drag the ball either way as he teased defenders and tempted them to lunge at him. He liked to wait until a defender had committed himself and then he wriggled away. Fulham developed his early talent for showmanship and after scoring 22 goals for them in 63 League matches he moved to QPR in 1966. The following year he scored one of the goals as Third Division Rangers beat WBA 3–2 in the first League Cup final at Wembley.

He spent six years at Rangers, scoring at the rate of a goal every other game, and helped the club reach the First Division. He had a cultish following at Loftus Road and there was much wailing and gnashing of teeth when the Manchester City manager Malcolm Allison swooped to take him to Maine Road for £200,000 in 1972. He spent four years weaving his magic and trying to halt the decline at City. He won the first of nine England caps and had his attitude been a little more disciplined he would have enjoyed a longer international career, but he was a flamboyant character who seemed unable to repeat his club form at international level. He obviously felt secure and confident playing in front of the same adoring audience week after week but what he couldn't do was transfer his talent successfully to another context.

Marsh was unable to play to his potential in a one-off situation against defenders who were likely to be just a little bit sharper than those he usually faced. At club level you can afford to follow a good game with an indifferent game because within a few days you get another chance to rectify the situation. At international level, with matches sometimes months apart, you have to turn in a reasonably good performance each time you play. I think Rodney found that transition difficult. He wasn't the fastest of strikers and he liked time to play with the ball. Foreign defenders, used to man-to-man marking, don't stand on ceremony. The fact that a player is an entertainer

Rodney Marsh (striker)
Hatfield 11.10.44
Fulham, Queen's Park Rangers,
Manchester City
England – 9

makes no difference to them. You don't get the same opportunity to do your tricks at international level, and I think Rodney probably suffered because of that.

He finished his playing career in England at Fulham in 1976 and then took his talent off to Tampa Bay in Florida where he helped to establish the game in the States.

They loved him there, just as they loved him wherever else he played. The advantage he had in America was that he was a good communicator, despite deafness in one ear. As a player you never knew which ear he was deaf in. I always assumed it was the one closest to the referee!

The Bohemian Rodney Marsh, shirt flapping outside his shorts as he dribbles his way through the defence, went on to contribute to the establishment of soccer in the USA.

STANLEY MATTHEWS

I didn't see much football on television as a child but the little I remember always seemed to feature Stanley Matthews. I've included him because as a youngster I remember him as a figurehead for the game. He was retiring just as I was joining West Ham as an apprentice but he must have had an enormous influence on a lot of impressionable young players at the time. Of course, the game when he played it was totally different from what it is today and people will always ask whether he would have been able to take on players and find the same sort of space in the modern game. The answer to that is no, but because of his level of skill and ability I'm sure he would have adapted to the demands of football in whatever era he played. I've often asked Stanley what made him such an outstanding player in his day. He thinks that his great strength was his speed over the first 10 yards, which is what he worked hardest at in training. He reckoned he could beat any defender from a standing start over 10 yards and that, of course, is what carried him into the open spaces and made him such an eye-catching player.

He was one of the game's first true superstars and it was unfortunate for him that he played most of his career during the era of the maximum wage, which was abolished in 1960 when his career was coming to a close. I can't help wondering what a player of his skill and stature would have earned in

Sir Stanley Matthews CBE
(winger)
Hanley 1.12.15
Stoke City, Blackpool
England – 54

The dribbling and crossing skills of Stanley Matthews, football's first-ever knight, remain an example to all. His match-winning display in the 1953 Cup final lives on in many memories.

today's game and what he would be worth on the transfer market. Were Stanley playing now he would be one of the game's genuine crowd-pleasers, one of the highest earners and the subject of the biggest transfer deals. He had the individual skill to unlock defences, and these days that is a priceless commodity in the game – one for which clubs pay enormous transfer fees. If he were playing today for an English club he would be earning in excess of £100,000 a year and, of course, if he were with one of the big Italian or Spanish clubs he would expect to be earning around £250,000 a year. Who knows what he would have been worth in the transfer market ... one million, two million, three million? It's anyone's guess. I'm sure those sorts of figures are something he must reflect upon occasionally when he reads about the financial rewards enjoyed by today's big name players. Few, though, will survive in the memory like Sir Stanley Matthews. He became one of the sport's great ambassadors, known and respected throughout the world, and he was the first player to be knighted for his services to professional football.

I remember bumping in to him in Mexico during the 1986 World Cup when he was there for a month as a guest of the World Cup sponsors to help them with their public relations. His reputation is such that wherever he is he can walk into a room full of football people and they know immediately that he is the soccer knight from England. I saw him again at a dinner in London in 1987. At the age of 72 he looked as fit as ever and told me that he still enjoys the occasional kick-about in Canada where he now lives. He told me how delighted he was to have recovered from a cartilage operation in six weeks. He reckoned it would have taken him several months to get over the same operation when he was a professional.

I think it's a shame that we no longer encourage the sort of wing play that became Stanley's trademark. He was a winger in the traditional sense, hugging the line, teasing the full back, pushing the ball past him, dashing after it and hitting a cross. I've seen him do that so many times in recordings of the 1953 FA Cup final that became known as the Matthews final and still gets a regular airing on television. He had received two runners-up medals when he achieved a lifetime's ambition, helping Blackpool to beat Bolton 4–3 at Wembley. In the film of that game you can appreciate his wonderful ball control, body swerve and pace.

He and Tom Finney were the great wingers of that time. Finney's career ended in 1959 and although I was very aware of him as a child I never saw him play and, for me, he didn't quite have the magic of Matthews. There are many, though, who feel Finney was the better player. Matthews was essentially an outside right; Finney was two footed, could play with equal ease on either wing and also appeared at centre forward. They were wing partners in at least 20 England teams. It was Stanley, though, who became revered as the wizard of dribble. The son of a professional boxer he started his career with his home town club, Stoke, then played for Blackpool before finishing his career back at Stoke. He played professionaly until he was 50 and I think the pace of the game would make that impossible these days.

MICK MILLS

I've included few full backs in my 100 players, not because there is any shortage of quality among players in this position, but because my favourite entertainers in the game are mostly midfield players or forwards, but I can't ignore Mick Mills. His consistency over 20 years was remarkable and, although not naturally gifted, during my England days he was probably the most reliable full back I played alongside. As far as retaining a sense of composure was concerned, he was almost in a league of his own. He was what many foreigners consider to be the typical English footballer – strong, quiet and unflappable. What always impressed me about him, too, was his ability to read the play and anticipate the development of dangerous situations. Although primarily right footed, he wore the number two and number three shirts with equal distinction and could also play the holding role in midfield.

He came from Godalming and was an apprentice at Portsmouth until they disbanded their youth scheme because of financial difficulties in 1966. Ipswich snapped him up and put him in their youth side. I remember playing against him several times in youth games as a youngster at Upton Park. Ipswich had a good young side in those days, but Mick was the best of the bunch. We eventually played together in the same England Youth squad. He was always a formidable tackler, likely to win the ball and surge forward for a shot at goal – he scored occasionally, too. He played in midfield in those days, so we clashed frequently. I respected him as a difficult opponent and I usually left the field after 90 minutes knowing I'd had a hard game. It was obvious, even then, that Mick was destined for greater things, and in 1965–66 he made his League debut, the same season that I made mine. He spent 18 seasons in the Ipswich first team and holds the record for the most League appearances for the club – 591. He was still learning the game when he played in the Ipswich side that won the Second Division championship in 1968, but by the time he led Bobby Robson's side to victory over Arsenal in the 1978 FA Cup final he was one of the most accomplished defenders in the world.

He was not particularly tall for a defender, but stocky, deceptively quick and hard in the tackle. He had a squat, bulldog build and would snap away at the heels of opponents. When he won the ball he didn't over-elaborate; he could use the ball well, but he was aware of his limitations. It was his determination and the fact that he encouraged by example that made him such an effective captain. He was given the responsiblity of coaxing the best out of the likes of Arnold Muhren and Frans Thijssen and encouraging emerging youngsters like Terry Butcher, Russell Osman and John Wark. The fact that this Ipswich team was so successful was due in no small measure to the leadership qualities displayed by Mills. With him at the helm, they finished third in Division One in 1980 and were runners-up in 1981 and 1982. But the crowning glory for that team, and a wonderful

Mick Mills MBE (full back)
Godalming 4.1.49
Ipswich Town, Southampton,
Stoke City
England – 42

169

climax, too, for Robson before taking over as England manager, came in May 1981 when they beat AZ 67 Alkmaar to win the UEFA Cup.

Mick's own moment of glory came the following year when Ron Greenwood, about to make way for Robson as England manager, made him captain of the World Cup squad because of injury to Kevin Keegan. He was a popular choice among the England lads and played throughout the World Cup, winning his 42nd and final cap in the goalless draw against Spain in Madrid. He was 33 by then and, although Robson took charge of the side, Mick didn't play for England again. Shortly after the World Cup he joined Keegan at Southampton where he gave excellent service under Lawrie McMenemy's management. He was again an influential figure as Southampton finished runners-up to Liverpool for the First Division title in 1983–84. He was a shrewd player with a good football brain and it was no surprise to me when he switched successfully to player–manager with Stoke City.

The unflappable Mick Mills was at home in both full back roles and a fine leader: he took over from the injured Kevin Keegan as captain of England during the 1982 World Cup.

BOBBY MOORE

Bobby was the supreme defender of his era. He was captain of West Ham and England and led by example – he wasn't the ranting and raving type. In all the years I've known Bobby I've never seen anything rattle him. In the dressing room he followed a meticulous pre-match preparation routine and he was almost obsessively tidy. He folded his clothes neatly and that was how he played – in a cool, calm, neat and tidy manner. Whenever West Ham travelled he had a hotel room to himself because he hated untidiness. He couldn't stand the mess another person might make. Someone like me sharing a hotel room with him would have been a disaster!

Bobby's distribution of the ball was impeccable. He developed a wonderful understanding at West Ham with Johnny Byrne, Geoff Hurst and Martin Peters, and their partnership provided the hard core of the 1966 World Cup winning team. Moore was so accomplished a passer that he would invariably drop the ball in an area furthest from the defender on the strongest side of a team-mate so that he could control it easily and effectively. He rarely hit a pass that was intercepted and the late Jimmy Bloomfield, a fine player and respected manager himself, once told me that Moore was the only player he had ever seen go through a 90 minute match without making a single mistake.

I believe Bobby was the player who was largely responsible for introducing to the English game the type of defender who made a positive

Bobby Moore OBE (centre back)
Barking 12.4.41
West Ham United, Fulham
England – 108

One of the best defenders England have produced since the war, Bobby Moore won a record 108 caps for England and was, of course, captain of that historic World Cup-winning England team of 1966.

171

attacking contribution. He had a marvellous gift of being able to use the ball constructively from deep positions and I think that he is the best English defender I've seen for knocking passes in to front strikers. Bobby was a late developer but he was so ambitious and dedicated that long serving members of the West Ham coaching staff still relate stories of how diligently he worked on the training pitch.

He signed for West Ham in 1958, won numerous England caps at youth level and made his senior debut in Peru in 1962. It was the start of an illustrious international career that was ultimately to earn him global acclaim as captain of the 1966 World Cup winning team and a record 108 England appearances. Whether he would have enjoyed the same opportunities had the outstanding Duncan Edwards survived the Munich air disaster in 1958 no one can know. My own feeling is that Bobby was such a talented defender, such a master of his craft, that he would have held off all challenges.

Apart from his distribution of the ball, he has to be one of the best readers of the game I've seen. His anticipation often meant that he was able to stifle attacks before they became a threat and this ability to forsee what was going to happen compensated for a lack of pace and meant that very few players were ever able to expose him. He always seemed to know what his opponent was going to do so he could time his tackling to perfection. He wasn't the greatest of headers, but when it was needed he was up there among the big men battling for the high balls. I think he was fantastic throughout the 1966 World Cup tournament and when he lifted the trophy at Wembley he was rightly acknowledged as the game's finest defender. It was a position he held for the rest of the decade with West Germany's Franz Beckenbauer the only other defender coming close to him.

Bobby spent 15 glorious years at Upton Park, winning the FA Cup, European Cup-winners' Cup and Footballer of the Year trophies, before joining Fulham in 1973. I remember how strange it felt playing for West Ham against him in the 1975 FA Cup final. I often wonder what would have happened had he been in the England side that played Poland in that fateful World Cup qualifying tie at Wembley two years earlier – a match that England had to win. Norman Hunter, who had played in the previous international (a 7–0 win over Austria) kept Bobby out of the side. At one stage in the game, Norman, perhaps trying to play the Moore style a little too casually, made a crucial error that allowed Lato to break away and set up a goal for Domarski. The match ended 1–1 and England failed to qualify for the 1974 World Cup. The writing was on the wall for Ramsey and, in a sense, for Moore, too. He played only one more game for England but he will always be remembered as one of the greatest of all England players. He was fortunate to be around at a time when the game was booming – a boom that he was partly responsible for. I think that he enjoyed being a celebrity in the 1960s and his blond hair, good looks and popular appeal made him a much sought-after personality at a time when soccer had a positive image.

ALAN MULLERY

I have often thought how difficult it must have been for a player joining Tottenham after they had won the fabled League and FA Cup double in 1961. That was a hard act to follow, yet Alan Mullery went to White Hart Lane three years later and proved himself to be one of the most durable and consistent midfield players in the club's history. Manager Bill Nicholson's wonderful side of 1961 set a very high standard, but Mullery met the challenge head-on, which was typical of the man. He was a good, old fashioned, all-round wing half, one of those committed, whole-hearted players who was totally reliable week after week. He came from Notting Hill and was built like a pocket battleship. He learned the basics of the game at Fulham, but really came to prominence with his transfer from Craven Cottage to White Hart Lane.

At Tottenham he slotted into the right half position vacated by Danny Blanchflower, who by that time had acquired something approaching legendary status. Not surprisingly Mullery took a little time to stamp his authority on the team, but it was soon apparent that his driving aggression would be a key factor in the years to come. He spent eight years at Spurs, collecting an FA Cup-winners' medal in 1967. Three seasons earlier he had won the first of 35 England caps, making his debut against Holland in Amsterdam. I think he reached the peak of his career in 1970 when he was an influential member of the side Sir Alf Ramsey took to Mexico to defend the World Cup. Although the 1966 team has secured its place in the history books by winning the World Cup, the 1970 side was just as good in my opinion, though it will always be remembered for losing the Cup.

Mullery's presence in the Nobby Stiles role, gave England a few extra options in midfield; he could tackle with the same purpose and diligence as Stiles and he had more to offer in the attacking sense. He proved his tremendous fitness and versatility in the heat of Mexico that summer and was probably one of England's most impressive players. He did a wonderful job against Brazil, marking the incomparable Pele, and against West Germany, when his attacking power was needed, he surged forward. He scored a super goal in that game, hitting a long shot in full stride. He was the sort of player who relished a challenge; he must have been an inspirational captain for Tottenham and a very encouraging influence in the dressing room before matches. He returned to Fulham in 1972 and I clearly remember one of the closing chapters of his playing career because I was involved in it – he was captain of the Fulham side that played West Ham in the 1975 FA Cup final.

He and Bobby Moore both played for Fulham that day and, in the period immediately before the match, I can remember pondering the rather intimidating prospect of facing two former giants of the England side in my first Wembley Cup final. West Ham won 2–0 but Mullery had a solid game, imposing himself on the midfield and using his vast store of experience

Alan Mullery MBE (midfield)
Notting Hill 23.11.41
Fulham, Tottenham Hotspur
England – 35

in an effort to open our defence. He had a very good knowledge of the game – as was later proved in his varied management career – and he had a very lively and amiable personality off the field. His strength as a player was his indomitable spirit. He was one of those players a manager could send out week after week safe in the knowledge that he would always produce his best.

Alan Mullery's driving aggression met the challenge of stepping into Danny Blanchflower's shoes at Tottenham, not to mention that of marking Pele in the 1970 World Cup.

PETER OSGOOD

Peter Osgood's name was synonymous with the excitement and flair of Chelsea in the 1970s. In those days Stamford Bridge was one of the most glamorous soccer arenas in Europe and Osgood, living his King's Road image to the hilt, was the club's most glamorous player. Chelsea was a team laden with personalities but none was as vibrant, as admired or as fêted as Osgood. He was an extrovert but his popularity with the Chelsea supporters was based on the outstanding ability he had as a centre forward and goalscorer. He had a natural talent and could have achieved so much more in the game had he adopted a more mature attitude to his fame.

Born in Windsor, he was already a very confident young man when he joined Chelsea as a junior in 1964. As a youngster he was a potentially brilliant player and although there were times later in his career when he reached the highest levels of the game he couldn't sustain his brilliance. He was mainly right footed – but what a right foot! When the ball was knocked up to him his control was almost instant. He could twist and turn his way out of tight situations with casual elegance. He was a lovely player to watch. Although more than 6 ft tall he wasn't the bulldozing type of centre forward. He had all the little tricks that you associate more readily with smaller strikers and he led the forward line with skill and inventiveness.

Peter Osgood (striker)
Windsor 20.2.47
Chelsea, Southampton,
Norwich City
England – 4

'Ossie the Wizard' vies with Southampton's John McGrath in 1971. The much-fêted Peter Osgood was a vibrant, elegant striker, the outstanding star in Chelsea's galaxy.

Like all good players, he was always aware of what was going on around him.

In nine seasons at Chelsea he scored 103 goals in 276 matches. Some of those goals were truly spectacular and around Stamford Bridge he became known as Ossie the Wizard. They were heady years at Chelsea and Ossie made the most of them. Looking back, I wonder how well he coped with the personality cult that developed around him. He had a rebellious, unpredictable character and after helping Chelsea to win the FA Cup against Leeds in 1970 and the European Cup-winners' Cup against Real Madrid in Athens a year later, his relationship with the club's rather scholarly manager, Dave Sexton, began to deteriorate.

Strangely, West Ham played a critical role in bringing about the eventual departure from Chelsea of their two most famous glamour boys, Osgood and the younger Alan Hudson, who as well as being team-mates, were close friends off the field. They were both in the Chelsea side that faced my old club at Stamford Bridge on Boxing Day 1973. West Ham were in a bit of relegation trouble (which was nothing new at the time) and after a first half in which Osgood and Hudson were outstanding we were trailing 2–0. Ron Greenwood, then West Ham's manager, tried to lift us during the interval but we went out for the second half knowing that something dramatic would have to happen for us to rescue the situation. Well, after a couple of minutes, Osgood had a chance around our penalty spot. He hit a superb volley and, fortunately for us, it struck our crossbar and bounced back to earth outside the 18-yard box. Our striker Bobby Gould immediately booted the ball upfield to relieve the pressure and Clyde Best ran onto the ball, outpacing two defenders, before scoring. The incident transformed the game and we ended up winning 4–2. Sexton dropped Osgood and Hudson from the team for the following game and that was the beginning of the end for both of them at Stamford Bridge. Osgood was sold to Southampton three months later for £275,000 after a series of bitter public rows with Sexton. It was an unhappy way in which to end his ten-year association with the club that had made him a household name and an England international.

He was a wonderfully gifted player and in my opinion would have won far more than four England caps had his attitude been more professional. For all his skill, he really wasn't Sir Alf Ramsey's cup of tea and his move to Southampton effectively ended any hopes he might have had of reviving his international career. He spent four years at the Dell as a valuable member of Lawrie McMenemy's squad, although he never recaptured the golden days at Chelsea. However, he played in the memorable 1976 FA Cup final win over Manchester United and in November of that year began a brief spell with Norwich. He later played for Philadelphia Furies in the United States before returning to Chelsea in 1978. My old West Ham team-mate Geoff Hurst, then Chelsea manager, signed him but by this time the great days for Osgood were long gone. He was welcomed as a returning hero but after 10 games and a row with Hurst he was shown the door.

TERRY PAINE

Eleven years after Terry Paine's retirement in 1977 he still held the record among outfield players for the most appearances in the Football League. In a marvellous 20-year career he played a total of 824 League matches – 713 for Southampton and 111 for Hereford. I played against him on many occasions and can't say that I ever looked forward to it, but I can't let that detract from the fact that he had a distinguished and rewarding reign as one of the best and most adaptable wingers in the modern game. He didn't endear himself to many of his opponents because he was a provocative type of player who spent a lot of time niggling and moaning. There's no doubt, either, that he had a ruthless streak in his game that meant he could be an uncompromising tackler but, as someone who played against him regularly, I had to respect his durability, consistency and skill on the field.

Born in Winchester, he was an orthodox winger when he joined Southampton from Winchester City in February 1957. He collected a Third Division championship medal in 1960 and three years later won the first of his 19 England caps. By now, of course, Alf Ramsey was in charge of the England team and was beginning to evolve a system of playing without wingers. It was with Ramsey's 'wingless wonders' that England won the World Cup in 1966. So Paine, in common with many other good young wingers at that time, such as Ian Callaghan and Johnny Giles, had to change his game.

It says something for his character that he buckled down to the challenge and accepted the new demands made on wide midfield players. He seemed to thrive on the fetching and carrying role that had become the burden of the modern midfield player. Ramsey appreciated Terry's industry, but he was never an automatic choice for the England side. He played once during the 1966 World Cup finals, against Mexico wearing Alan Ball's number seven shirt, and that, as it turned out, was his last international appearance. If he was disappointed at missing out on the greatest day in England's soccer history, he was able to console himself with a major domestic triumph that season. He was an influential member of the Southampton side – scoring 16 goals in 40 matches – that finished runners-up in Division Two and climbed into Division One for the first time in the club's history.

I will always remember him for his long sideburns and slick, black hair, but Micky Channon remembers him for the enormous influence he had on the youngsters at the Dell. Channon, an England colleague of mine, played alongside Paine in the Southampton side for about seven years and gives him a lot of credit for his own progress at the Dell. Paine felt it was part of his responsibility to help bring the club's youngsters through the youth ranks. I can imagine him providing a good example to youngsters on the training pitch because he was fast, tricky, two footed and essentially a creative player who wanted to win.

In his 713 League games for Southampton he scored 160 goals, which

Terry Paine MBE (midfield)
Winchester 23.3.39
Southampton, Hereford United
England – 19

is approximately one every four games – a remarkable scoring rate for a winger converted to a midfield player. He spent 17 years at the Dell and when he left to become player–coach at Hereford in August 1974 it was as though an era in the club's history had come to a close. Paine was 34 at the time, still an influential player bristling with purpose, and Hereford, elected to the Football League only two years previously, needed his experience and wisdom. They had already secured a place in Division Three and, with Paine directing operations in midfield, they duly won the Third Division title in 1975–76. Paine played 40 matches that season and, against Peterborough in October, played the 765th League game of his career, beating the all-time League appearance record held by Portsmouth's Jimmy Dickinson (1946–65). Paine's career ended the following season at the age of 37. He played 26 League games as Hereford found the Second Division too tough for them and were relegated. The last game of his extraordinary career was played in May 1977, ironically against Southampton.

Terry Paine began his 17-year career at Southampton as a winger, but then successfully switched to midfield where he achieved a remarkable average of one goal every four games.

STEVE PERRYMAN

Someone once described Steve as a 'babyfaced killer' which might sound a bit dramatic but wasn't entirely inappropriate in the football sense. He always had a youthful, boyish appearance which tended to disguise the quite formidable character which lay beneath the surface. He was a tenacious opponent, as I experienced many times, a diligent marker and a powerful tackler who had little time for the niceties of the game once the referee blew the whistle for the kick-off. We quite often competed against each other in the big West Ham–Spurs derby matches and I received a few momentoes of his tackling on my legs. I knew that whenever I played against him he would try to deny me time and space and it was up to me to make the time and get the space. I can't remember him once giving less than 100 per cent.

He had a neat, compact build and looked like a primary schoolboy when he got into the Spurs first team at the age of 18 in 1969. In those days he was a ball winning midfield player, but he later showed his versatility by playing a central defensive role and finally at right back. He used the ball intelligently and was fortunate not to have too many long term injuries, but he was always just short of being considered for international recognition. He did get one cap, though, during the build-up to the 1982 World Cup in Spain. Ron Greenwood, the England manager, had organised two warm-up games on the same evening immediately before the squad departed for Spain. The first eleven played in Finland the second eleven played in Iceland. Steve went to Iceland and came on as a substitute in a 1–1 draw.

One of the reasons why Steve failed to make a breakthrough on the international scene was his versatility as a player. This is always a problem for players who are not specialists in one position. Tottenham used his ability to fulfil several roles to their own advantage and, although Steve didn't complain, I think it probably cost him recognition as an outstanding player in one position. He was an all-rounder and Spurs would call upon him to fill gaps in the side left by injury or suspension. I felt he came closest to breaking into the England side towards the end of his career at Spurs when he was settled at right back but, by then, Liverpool's Phil Neal was well established in the number two shirt.

He was probably one of the most successful Spurs players since the double side of 1961 and something of a rarity in that he progressed – like Glenn Hoddle – through the youth scheme at White Hart Lane. Tottenham's tradition is to spend big money on players in the transfer market. This was a major factor in helping me to make up my mind about which club to join when they invited me along to train with them as a youngster. For Steve to break through as early as he did, to become such an inspirational and influential captain and to make a club record 655 League appearances, was a marvellous achievement.

Among his many honours were two FA Cup final wins, two appearances

Steve Perryman MBE
(*midfield*)
Ealing 21.12.51
Tottenham Hotspur, Oxford United, Brentford
England – 1

Steve Perryman, the 'babyfaced killer'. Although in his early years at Spurs he was a ball-winning midfielder, his tremendous versatility later led to a variety of roles.

in the UEFA Cup final and the Footballer of the Year award in 1982. He finished his playing career with Oxford and Brentford and then went into management at Griffin Park. In 1988, approaching his thirty-seventh year, he was still fulfilling the dual role of player–manager with Brentford and was poised to join the élite group of professionals who have played in 1,000 first team games.

MARTIN PETERS

West Ham supporters still look back on England's 1966 World Cup winning team affectionately as their own because of the immense contribution made by Bobby Moore, Geoff Hurst and Martin Peters. The famous Upton Park trio are invariably referred to in that order with Martin the third in line, almost as an afterthought. I suppose they have to be remembered in some sort of sequence though it has always struck me as slightly unfair to Martin. In a sense, though, the order in which they are still fondly recalled reflects their responsibilities. Bobby was captain of England and a very self-assured celebrity in the 1960s and 1970s; Geoff, the hat trick hero, was buoyant and confident, and Martin was the most reserved of the three. He went about his work very quietly, but with great pride and sense of purpose.

There was no show or extravagance about Martin. He could have become the forgotten man but, in my opinion, his football ability should secure him a lasting place in the game's history books. The goals he created – including numerous ones for Geoff, as he would be the first to admit – and those he scored himself stamped him as a player of the highest class, combining a wonderful eye for an opening with the knack of sneaking unseen into the opposing penalty area for scoring attempts. Those in the game were very aware of his ability. Sir Alf Ramsey was one of his greatest admirers and once described him as a player '10 years ahead of his time', a phrase that was to stick with Martin throughout his playing career. He was probably one of the most versatile players of his generation. He wore all 11 shirts for West Ham, including the goalkeeper's jersey. In his early days this could have inhibited his development a little because, when there was an injury, he was invariably the player who had to fill in at full back or centre back. In different circumstances he might have developed into more of a specialist. His versatility was also one of his great strengths. He was an invaluable member of Ramsey's squad, winning 67 caps – the first just before the 1966 World Cup – in an eight-year international career.

As a schoolboy I remember watching Martin play in the West Ham side that lost 8–2 to Blackburn Rovers in 1963–64. It was at Christmas and Martin lost his place to Eddie Bovington for the return match two days later. This time, West Ham won 3–1 at Blackburn and, as a result, Eddie kept his place in the side for the next couple of months and played in the 1964 FA Cup final against Preston at Martin's expense. But two years later, with form and flair rediscovered, Martin was one of the wide midfield players in Ramsey's 'wingless wonders'. Naturally right footed, he played up and down the left flank using his creativity and vision to open opposing defences. He was a brave, athletic, reliable player and Ramsey kept faith with him until the end of his managerial reign. I made my international debut in Alf's last match in Portugal in April 1974 and Martin was captain that day, playing the anchor role in the centre of midfield.

Martin scored 80 goals in 300 games for West Ham, which is a very

Martin Peters MBE (midfield)
Plaistow 8.11.43
West Ham United, Tottenham
Hotspur, Norwich City,
Sheffield United
England – 67

The brave Martin Peters in action for Spurs, the club he joined in 1970. A member of England's celebrated West Ham trio in the 1966 World Cup, he scored the second goal in that breathtaking victory over West Germany in the final.

good return for a midfield player. He was a subtle player with a fine touch and would ghost unnoticed into the penalty box to score at the back post. In 1970 he became Britain's first £200,000 rated player, when he moved to Tottenham as Jimmy Greaves went in the opposite direction as part of the deal. He spent five years at Tottenham where he relished the challenge of European club football, winning a UEFA Cup-winners' medal in 1972.

He was always sparely built – even today he looks as though he could play for 90 minutes – and, despite a troublesome Achilles' tendon injury, he gave full value during the closing chapters of his careeer with Norwich and Sheffield United. Of course, he never surpassed that great day in 1966 when, at the age of 22, he scored in the World Cup final. Few players ever achieve such distinction but, typically, even on his big day, his glory was diluted somewhat by his two West Ham team-mates. Geoff Hurst scored the hat trick, Bobby Moore lifted the World Cup, and Martin got the other goal.

KEVIN RATCLIFFE

Since the re-emergence of Everton as a major force in the First Division no one has impressed me more at Goodison Park than Kevin Ratcliffe. For me, he has been the key player in their success. People have tended to take him for granted but I suspect that's because of his consistency. Few players can have gained so much respect from within the game as unobtrusively. Ratcliffe was born in Mancot and played in the same Flintshire schools side as Ian Rush. They grew up together, they share a room on Welsh international trips and they could have gone to Chester together as apprentices.

Kevin Ratcliffe (centre back)
Mancot 12.11.60
Everton
Wales – 43

Rush chose Chester as the launching pad for his career but Ratcliffe, an Everton supporter as a schoolboy, stayed true to his favourite club and went to Goodison Park as an apprentice, signing professional forms in 1978. There was a time when he might have regretted that decision. He flitted in and out of the first team as a left back, and when he asked for a transfer the manager Howard Kendall implored him to stay and decided to try him at centre back. As it turned out, that was a masterstroke. Ratcliffe came into the side for the unfortunate Mark Higgins, a promising central defender who sustained a serious injury that cut short his career.

Kevin played intermittently between 1980 and 1983 and didn't play a full season until 1983–84, by which time he was 23 and already a fixture alongside Rush in the Wales team. When Higgins was injured that season Ratcliffe took over the captaincy and, after a disastrous string of results when Kendall looked as though he might get the sack, the team suddenly found some form. At the end of that season Ratcliffe lifted the FA Cup at Wembley after the 2–0 win over Watford. He also played in the Milk Cup final against Liverpool – and Rush – but this time finished on the losing side. And, having been threatened with relegation at Christmas, Everton ended the season in seventh place.

Since then Ratcliffe has become the calming influence in both the Everton and Wales teams. Everton's game is built on a very sound defensive system and Ratcliffe's role is crucial. They have developed the Liverpool style of possession football and they play a very tight and rigid offside game, particularly when they are away from home. But there are perhaps three or four occasions in every game when the opposition breaks through and, on most of those instances, the sense of anticipation allied to Ratcliffe's astonishing speed is sufficient to snuff out the danger. If a striker breaks clear of the Everton back four the chances are that Ratcliffe will make up the ground and get a tackle in within 10 yards. Few other First Division defenders possess his pace.

He's sturdily built and the way he plays reminds me a great deal of Colin Todd, a former Everton defender. I was a great admirer of Todd and would put Ratcliffe in the same class. He's strong in the tackle and although not tall for a centre back Everton are rarely exposed in the air in the heart of their defence. He's not as constructive as Alan Hansen, for instance, but still darts forward on occasions to support his attack. He's also got a little ruthless streak that means he can't be intimidated.

His leadership qualities were crucial in Everton's championship winning seasons of 1985 and 1987. He also helped them to three consecutive FA Cup finals (1984–86) and played in the side that beat Rapid Vienna 3–1 in the European Cup-winners' Cup final in Rotterdam in May 1985. As manager of Wales, Mike England would regularly enthuse over Ratcliffe's influence on his side. He made him captain of Wales and while Rush may have dominated the headlines there is no doubt that those within the game recognised that Ratcliffe's contribution was substantial. He has now made more than 40 appearances for his country and I can honestly say that I can't remember seeing him play a bad game for either Wales or Everton.

A key player in Howard Kendall's successful Everton side, Kevin Ratcliffe's anticipation and speed were a feature of his defensive qualities.

JOHN ROBERTSON

I have always considered John Robertson to be one of the key figures in the success of Brian Clough at Nottingham Forest. John was an unlikely looking winger, but he had a purple patch in the 1970s when he really was one of the most dangerous wingers in the First Division, if not in Europe. I think it's fair to say that when he emerged from the apprentice ranks at Nottingham he was a stooping, slightly overweight reserve team player whom few had recognised as a potential match winner. He made his League debut in 1971 and two years later had established himself as a first team regular, but it wasn't until Clough arrived as manager from Leeds in January 1975 that John's career really began to take shape. Along with other players like Larry Lloyd, John McGovern, Kenny Burns and Tony Woodcock, Robertson began to repay the faith Clough had shown in him.

Short and stocky, he was a winger who hugged the touchline and gave Forest the width they needed to stretch defences. I have never known a winger play as wide as John. He ran shoulder to shoulder with the linesman and if the rules had allowed him to stray off the pitch he would have done so. He played on the left side and a high percentage of Forest's attacks were created by him. Knowing that, and even knowing his strengths and weaknesses, it was still impossible to subdue him completely. When West Ham were about to meet Forest in the late 1970s his was usually the first name mentioned in the team-talk and when we dragged ourselves back into the dressing room after 90 minutes we were usually still mumbling, 'How do you stop that Robertson?'. His superb close control in tight situations was primarily what set him apart from other wingers. He wasn't especially quick over a long distance, but he had acceleration and a darting run and, most of all, he knew precisely when to release the ball.

I was always impressed with the understanding he seemed to enjoy with Woodcock and quite often he would knock the ball in to Tony, race down the wing to collect the return in full stride and then wriggle past the marking full back. His burst of acceleration gave him half a yard of space to get in his cross and he had the knack of curling his centres away from the hands of the goalkeeper. Even in the tightest situation, when faced by a full back and covering midfield player, he always seemed able to hit a high cross that was bending away from the goalkeeper. It was his endless stream of crosses from the left side of the field that regularly put First Division defences under pressure on Saturday afternoons throughout the 1970s. It was a Robertson cross from the left that gave Trevor Francis the chance to score with a rare header in the European Cup final against Malmö in Munich in 1979. The following year he was the goalscorer himself when Forest beat SV Hamburg 1–0 in the European Cup final in Madrid. Forest's domination of Europe began, of course, when they won the League title for the first time in 1977–78. John played in all 42 League games that season, scoring 12 goals in the best scoring season of his career. He also

John Robertson (winger)
Uddingston 20.1.53
Nottingham Forest, Derby County
Scotland – 28

played in two League Cup winning teams with Forest – against Liverpool in 1978 and Southampton in 1979.

John wasn't the most athletic looking player, nor the hardest working winger. If I have a criticism of him it has to be that he sometimes tended to overlook his defensive obligations. If he lost the ball, or a Forest attack broke down, he would tend to amble leisurely back. I played against him regularly and sometimes thought that he was about to drift out of the game altogether. But, once he had the ball at his feet, he was a different player. He compensated for a lack of endurance and sustained pace, by enticing defenders to commit themselves. Once they had lunged at him, he twisted and turned out of trouble and used the little space he had created to get in his cross.

He won 28 caps for Scotland but in my view he was rarely able to repeat his best Forest form, either on the international stage, or at Derby County, whom he joined in 1983. Brian Clough is often credited with having strong powers of motivation and I think John Robertson's career supports that theory; Brian knew how to get the best out of John and how to exploit his strengths. When John left Derby he went into non-League football with Corby and later moved to Grantham where he became coach under manager Martin O'Neill, his former playing colleague at Forest.

It was John Robertson's barrage of crosses from the left side of the field that regularly pressurised First Division defences on the Saturday afternoons of the 1970s.

186

BRYAN ROBSON

I remember Bryan well as a very ambitious and determined young player at West Bromwich Albion and after one particular game against him I sat in the dressing room thinking that here was a young man destined for great things. He became one of the outstanding midfield players of his generation but, sadly, injury has plagued the latter seasons of his career. In many ways Bryan is very similar to Kevin Keegan; I wouldn't describe either of them as naturally gifted players but, like Kevin, Bryan has succeeded because of his dedication to his profession. He has good all-round ability and, when fully fit, is one of the strongest and most athletic players in the world.

Bryan Robson (midfield)
Chester-le-Street 11.1.57
West Bromwich Albion,
Manchester United
England – 69

He is a jack-of-all-trades player; he has a crisp, clean touch on the ball and good awareness, but it's really his non-stop style of play that separates him from lesser men. He can tackle, work back and cover as well as any back four player. He gets through a prodigious amount of work in midfield and moves into scoring positions almost as often as a front striker. That's why Manchester United paid £1.5 million – then a record for a deal between British clubs – to Albion for his signature in October 1981.

Initially a back four player, he developed the attacking side of his game to such an extent that his powerful surges from midfield into the penalty area have now become his trademark. The timing of his runs has produced several important goals, none more notable than the first in England's opening World Cup tie against France in Spain in 1982 which came after just 20 seconds. That was a typical Robson goal; Steve Coppell took a quick throw-in on the right flank, deep in the French half, Terry Butcher headed the ball on and Robson was there, steaming into the penalty area, to score. Midway through the second half he scored another fine goal that illustrated perfectly his bravery as he plunged unhesitatingly in among the boots and studs to get his head to the ball.

He is almost recklessly courageous and, because of that, injuries are inevitable. The hamstring and shoulder injuries that plagued him for two years between 1985–87 were damaging not only to him but to England and Manchester United. Because of the way he plays, he needs to be fully fit and able to maximise his strength and running ability; he is not the type of player who can turn out only 75 per cent fit and still contribute significantly to the team effort. When he coasts he becomes an ordinary player.

As an observer at the 1986 World Cup in Mexico, and as a Robson fan who wanted him in the side, I felt strongly that he shouldn't have been selected to play because of his shoulder injury. He simply wasn't 100 per cent fit and capable of meeting the challenge of the World Cup. But Bryan was the captain and he felt that he had a responsibility to the team, and I could understand his insistence that he should play as I had been in a similar situation myself once with a groin injury. You cling to the hope that it will be okay and that some miracle will help get you through the 90 minutes, but that rarely works. Bryan wasn't fit in Mexico and an unfit captain, worried about damaging his shoulder again, wasn't going to be the inspiring player that England needed in those circumstances. It was a mistake to play him and a big anti-climax at a memorable stage of his career. He is still a wonderful player and I hope that he doesn't suffer any further serious injuries, but my own feeling is that in the next couple of years we will see him moving back into defence as his running ability inevitably fades.

The inspirational captain, Bryan Robson, was the only England player to show his true form in the 1988 European Championships — England's three consecutive defeats were a bitter disappointment to him.

IAN RUSH

Ian is a goalscoring phenomenon who became the most expensive footballer in British soccer history when the glamorous Italian club, Juventus, paid Liverpool £3.2 million pounds to secure his services. When he began his Italian career in the summer of 1987 he was poised to become the greatest goalscorer in the game and the soccer history books will rank him alongside the all-time greats, though when he went to Italy I still rated Jimmy Greaves just ahead of him. Ian was 25 when he left Liverpool and, injuries permitting, he has the time and the ability to overtake players like Greaves, Denis Law and Nat Lofthouse and become the most prolific marksman of all time. He began his career modestly enough with Chester and after two seasons there Liverpool signed him and, typically, kept him in the reserves for a year while he learned the subtleties of their game. In 1981 he made his debut for Liverpool and the following season won a regular first team place. With that came the goals, 17 in the League in 1981–82, 24 in 1982–83, 32 in 1983–84.

Predominantly right footed, his speed is his greatest strength. His control in tight situations is excellent and although he thrives on a good service from midfield, he has enough ability to create his own goalscoring chances. He has proved to be a most elusive opponent, practically impossible to mark well because of his anticipation, speed and the timing of his runs. He has to be one of the sharpest and most clinical finishers I've seen. In his seven seasons at Liverpool he benefited enormously from the guidance and influence of Kenny Dalglish, with whom he formed one of the most lethal striking partnerships in the First Division in the 1980s.

Sparely built and 6 ft 1 in tall, he has the physical prowess and the cunning to outwit most defenders and his composure when faced with a one-to-one situation against a goalkeeper gives him a better than average chance of scoring. At Anfield, where he inevitably became the hero of the terraces, he scored at the rate of a goal every other match, which is a quite extraordinary record in the modern game. His 23 goals were crucial in helping Liverpool to win the First Division title for a record sixteenth time in 1985–86. His darting runs in the final third of the field provided immense excitement for the Anfield fans and when Liverpool announced their decision to sell him the supporters pleaded with the club not to let him go.

It was easy to see why the Kop would miss Ian; a remarkable dimension to his goalscoring performance over his five and a half years there was that for the first 144 games in which he scored, Liverpool never lost. That incomparable record was prevented from being perfect when Ian's 202nd goal was overhauled by Arsenal with two goals from Charlie Nicholas in the 1987 Littlewoods Cup final. Ian also guided Liverpool to the runners-up position in the League, behind Everton, captaining the team in his final appearance at Anfield, typically getting the winner against Watford. He

Ian Rush (striker)
St Asaph 20.10.61
Chester City, Liverpool,
Juventus
Wales – 38

left English soccer after a 3–3 draw at Chelsea, scoring his 30th goal in the League that season and his 207th for the club.

He was born in St Asaph and, after making his international debut as a substitute against Scotland in 1980, became the central figure around whom Wales built their team. It would be fascinating to see Wales progress to the World Cup finals so that Rush could test himself on the the biggest stage in the game. The move to Juventus, where he had to come to terms with the man-to-man marking of the Italian game, provided him with a fresh and intriguing challenge – and financial security for life. Sadly, however, after the retirement of former French captain Michel Platini Rush no longer received the service that he needed. Initially, goals were sparse and Rush, as a foreign superstar, came under increasing pressure from the voracious Italian media as he tried to justify the huge transfer fee. But as long as he receives the support and service he enjoyed at Liverpool there is no reason why he shouldn't be just as successful as he was on Merseyside.

A goal-scoring phenomenon at Liverpool, Ian Rush found fewer opportunities to exercise his craft at Juventus.

KENNY SANSOM

Kenny was one of the most exciting young defenders I'd ever seen when he was at Crystal Palace. But, such was the impression that he made on me then that now I am sometimes disappointed that we don't see so many of the attacking sorties that were a feature of his early career. There is no question that he is a great left back but he showed such early potential that I was not alone in thinking that he would become the complete defender. He had a good grounding under the shrewd eye of Terry Venables in the Palace side that was tagged the 'team of the 1980s'.

Sansom, Billy Gilbert and Jerry Murphy, among other players, grew up together at Selhurst Park and won the FA Youth Cup a couple of times.

Kenny Sansom (full back)
Camberwell 26.9.58
Crystal Palace, Arsenal
England – 86

Kenny Sansom, an exciting, attacking left back dominated the position for England in the 1980s.

191

Kenny stood out in those days because of his speed and his overlapping attacking play. I remember playing with him in an England XI in a testimonial match at Aston Villa and I've never forgotten the electrifying runs he made from the left back position deep into the opposing half. He was like an orthodox left winger playing at left back and he obviously made an impression because in 1979 he made his debut in Ron Greenwood's team against Wales.

That season Kenny won a Second Division championship medal with Palace and after one more season at Selhurst Park he was transferred to Arsenal in a £1 million exchange deal involving Clive Allen. I felt Kenny stood still for a while at Arsenal, perhaps because they restricted his attacking play which was, after all, his greatest strength. I also felt that he needed to be careful with his weight because he's a chunky 5 ft 6 in and can't afford to carry excess weight. But by this time Kenny had established himself as a threat to Mick Mills in the England team though the Ipswich captain kept Ken out for a long period in 1981. Mills' form eventually won him the captaincy of the 1982 World Cup team in Spain though Greenwood decided to play him at right back which meant Kenny was reinstated at left back.

Since Bobby Robson took over after the 1982 World Cup Kenny has been virtually ever present in the England side. He is already the most capped full back in England's history and is well on his way to becoming one of the élite who have made 100 appearances. To his credit Kenny has never taken his domination of the left back spot for granted. He has continued to work hard to improve his game even though there had been no sustained challenge to him from any other left back until the emergence of Nottingham Forest's Stuart Pearce. He has improved his game defensively though I still think that sometimes his reading of the play lets him down. Going forward though, he would have few rivals if he could attack with the consistency he showed as a youngster. He is an amiable, chirpy extrovert character, good to have in the dressing room, but I suspect he now faces a fight to retain his England place following the disappointments of the 1988 European Championship.

PETER SHILTON

I think you have to put Peter Shilton in the same class as Gordon Banks and considering they came from the same school – Leicester City – I suppose that isn't surprising. Peter is a quite superb goalkeeper and, at his peak, was probably unrivalled. I first met him when we were both teenagers playing for the England Youth side against Scotland. He was a year younger than most of the rest of the team but, even in that situation, he had a very confident and dominant personality. Most newcomers to an international squad are a bit shy and take a little time to settle in, but Peter was immediately an impressive figure, particularly in training, shouting his orders and organising the free kicks. He played superbly in that match against the Scots and you had to admire his confidence.

Peter has always struck me as being a very ambitious person which I think was illustrated in his play and he had an air of arrogance that set him apart from so many of his contemporaries. Even as a youngster in the mid-1960s I can recall him trying to force the issue at Leicester City over Gordon Banks – telling the club that if he couldn't be first choice goalkeeper then he would leave. At the time Banks was England's World Cup goalkeeper, but Peter knew where he wanted to go and he knew how to get there. He has always had total belief in his own ability and is very diligent about his training; during the years we played together in the England side his training routines never changed or slackened. He can be moody but he never let that mar his training routine. He could get depressed by criticism or if his team had lost a game because of a mistake he had made; conceding a goal, even in training, was something he took as a personal failing. There were many times when I watched him thumping the training pitch in disgust and frustration because he had let a shot slip under his body.

In many ways Peter was unfortunate to have been around at the same time as Ray Clemence, who played 61 times for England. Alone and unchallenged, one or other of them would probably have ended up with about 150 caps. As it is, Peter has won more caps than any other England goalkeeper, long ago passing the legendary Banks' total of 73. He joined that élite group of internationals with 100 or more England caps – Bobby Moore, Bobby Charlton and Billy Wright – during the European Championships in West Germany in June 1988. He became the first England goalkeeper to win 100 caps in the 3–1 defeat against Holland in Düsseldorf, and as it was his intention to play on for at least a further two years, it was possible he would overtake the 119 international appearances by Pat Jennings of Northern Ireland.

What made him so reliable was his shot-stopping, which was his greatest strength. His reflexes were so good that he could reach almost any shot coming towards him. He was a wonderful technician and certainly the man for the young goalkeeper to watch and study. Throughout a game he

Peter Shilton MBE (goalkeeper)
Leicester 18.9.49
Leicester City, Stoke City,
Nottingham Forest,
Southampton, Derby County
England – 100

would talk, encourage, organise and tell his defenders who they should be picking up. He was a very dominant, demanding personality in his own penalty area. It was hard to pick out a weakness in his game though it was generally recognised that he was not as strong on crosses.

Playing against him in the First Division could be a chastening experience, but playing with him for England . . . well, there were times on foreign fields when Peter made a save that would win the match for us. On those occasions a good goalkeeper is as valuable as a good goalscorer. Peter was a perfectionist and sometimes you just had to let him do his own thing. In the dressing room before big matches he would get totally locked up in his own build-up. He always wanted the side to win but, for him, his own performance was perhaps more important. For that reason he would always go through a strenuous warm-up session before matches and during these he would be psyching himself up, too. He liked to build up a sweat beforehand because it was important to him that he was attuned to the pace of the game from the kick-off. Sometimes five or 10 minutes can elapse in a match before the goalkeeper has a significant touch of the ball, and Peter always wanted to be sure that, were he in that situation, he would at least be physically prepared for a sudden flurry of activity and not be caught cold.

In the summer of 1987, at the age of 37, he moved from Southampton to Derby County, who had recently been promoted to Division One. The transfer seemed to renew his appetite for the game and as the 1988 European Championship approached he was still unchallenged as England's number one goalkeeper. It was a difficult season for Derby, though, struggling to consolidate their position in Division One, but for Peter it was a season that carried him into the pages of the game's record books. In April 1988, in a 1–1 draw against Watford at Vicarage Road, he played the 825th League match of his career, surpassing Terry Paine's 11-year-old record. No player in the sport's history has appeared in more football League matches. On the day he broke the record he promised to play on for another two seasons so it could be that his career milestone will never be beaten.

OPPOSITE *Peter Shilton makes his debut for Stoke City in 1974. He was to become one of the greatest goalkeepers of all time, gaining his 100th cap in the 1988 European Championships.*

GRAEME SOUNESS

Graeme Souness (midfield)
Edinburgh 6.5.53
Tottenham Hotspur,
Middlesbrough, Liverpool,
Sampdoria, Glasgow Rangers
Scotland – 54

Throughout Graeme's career he has had the reputation of being rather rebellious – a reputation that has probably been quite justified. Even as an outstanding youngster at Tottenham, he walked out of White Hart Lane and returned home to Edinburgh partly because he was homesick and partly because he wasn't getting a chance in the first team. He always struck me as a confident, slightly arrogant player and I think this must have been apparent right from those early clashes with Bill Nicholson at Spurs. He had joined Tottenham as an apprentice and spent three years there without getting into the League side.

I think his behaviour and attitude to authority virtually forced the club to sell him and he went to Middlesbrough where he came under the wing of Jackie Charlton. It was probably Jack who found the way to approach Graeme and get the best out of him because he was very soon establishing himself as a midfield player of immense potential. He spent five years at Middlesbrough, playing around 200 matches. He refined his game a little and added the ability to hit a wonderful long pass to all his other qualities. He won the first of more than 50 Scottish caps in 1975 and by the time he moved to Liverpool three years later was one of the most accomplished midfield players in the game.

I think Liverpool provided the perfect platform for him. They were strong on discipline and professionalism and Graeme responded in the way they hoped, to such a degree in fact that he was eventually made captain. His passing ability, his touch, his tackling, his aggression and qualities of leadership became vital elements of Liverpool's continued domination of European football. He played in the European Cup final triumphs over FC Bruges in 1978, Real Madrid in 1981 and Roma in 1984. He was predominantly right footed though he compensated for this by being able to strike the ball equally well with the inside and outside of the foot and he scored some spectacular goals from long range. He seemed to become more aggressive at Liverpool and, I also felt, exuded an air of menace. He was involved in one or two unsavoury incidents – stamping on Peter Nicholas and elbowing Ray Wilkins.

Later in his career he played for Sampdoria in Italy but in future years will probably be best remembered, particularly in Scotland, for the way he rejuvenated Glasgow Rangers when appointed player–manager in 1986. In his first season they won the Scottish championship with a team he had completely rebuilt. Controversially, he had also signed several English players including Terry Butcher, Graham Roberts, Trevor Francis, Ray Wilkins and Chris Woods. Sadly, he was sent off twice in his first season at Rangers and although that controversial tag seemed to follow him everywhere it cannot detract from the fact that he was a superbly polished midfield player of great technical ability.

OPPOSITE *The determined face of Graeme Souness, a player who has sometimes made the headlines for the wrong reasons. I prefer to remember the wonderful passing and control that contributed so much to Liverpool's glory.*

NEVILLE SOUTHALL

I consider Neville to be one of the great modern goalkeeping heroes and his presence was one of the reasons why Everton won the First Division title in 1985 and again in 1987. At 6 ft 1 in and weighing in at 12 st, he has the ideal physique for a goalkeeper and with experience has come the positioning and awareness that now makes him an invaluable member of the Everton side. Born in Llandudno, he began his professional career with Bury whom he joined from Winsford in 1980. He had just one season in the Bury first team before Everton snapped him up. He was 23 before he got into the Everton first team which makes him quite a late developer, but he was soon to play a fundamental role in Everton's emergence from Liverpool's shadow. He is an economic goalkeeper who does the job very effectively, without any show or over-elaboration.

Neville Southall (goalkeeper)
Llandudno 16.9.58
Bury, Everton
Wales — 34

The last line of defence: Neville Southall always retains his sharpness for the full 90 minutes of the match.

Working for the BBC I saw a lot of Everton in their championship seasons of 1985 and 1987 and Neville frequently produced saves that proved to be the turning point of crucial matches. His anticipation is quite superb; he is a good shot-stopper and he has a very positive and determined attitude to the job. He has also displayed great courage on countless occasions, diving in amid a mass of boots to catch low crosses; lesser goalkeepers sometimes choose to stand on their line in such situations. Neville likes to be a dominant force and such is his sense of timing that he invariably wins the balls that he challenges for. Occasionally I feel he can be recklessly brave and that probably accounts for the fact that he has had more than his fair share of injuries.

Neville also likes to take the responsibility for organising his defence and I think it must be partly due to his direction that the Everton back four are rarely pushed into their own penalty area, thus enabling them to play such an effective offside trap. His aggressive attitude has occasionally brought him into conflict with referees and I always remember seeing him foolishly get himself sent off at Chelsea. Nonetheless, his contribution to Everton's success has been significant, a fact that was acknowledged with the Footballer of the Year award in 1985 and the first of many Wales caps in 1982.

As one of the great individual talents in the Welsh team, like Ian Rush, Mark Hughes and Kevin Ratcliffe, it is a pity that Neville has not yet had the opportunity to display his skills on the great stages of the World Cup and European Championships, nor been more rewarded with European club competition for Everton's domestic success during the ban on English clubs abroad.

MIKE SUMMERBEE

Mike Summerbee (winger)
Cheltenham 15.12.42
Swindon Town, Manchester
City, Burnley, Blackpool,
Stockport County
England – 8

Mike Summerbee was the working man's winger – not the talented individual who hugged the line waiting for the ball to arrive at his feet, but the willing racehorse who toiled for 90 minutes, went in search of the ball and was prepared to win it with a biting tackle when necessary. He was a good, skilful player and a ruthless streak in his make-up meant that he made an intimidating opponent.

He was a West Country boy from a footballing family. His uncle, George, had been a professional with Chester, Preston and Barrow and when Mike left school he played for his home town club, Cheltenham, until Swindon spotted his potential. Their manager at the time, Bert Head, was making a habit of producing good, young players – Ernie Hunt, Bobby Woodruff, Don Rogers and Rod Thomas come to mind – but Mike was probably the best of the bunch. He played more than 200 games for Swindon, helping them to clinch the runners-up spot in Division Three in 1963. Inevitably, his dashing excursions along the flanks caught the eye of some of the bigger clubs and in August 1965 Manchester City paid £30,000 to sign him – and what a bargain he turned out to be. Joining City at the time Alf Ramsey was beginning to dispense with wingers on the international scene, Summerbee quickly adapted to the demands being made on the new breed of midfield flank men.

Primarily right footed, he made an immediate impression at Maine Road with his industry and diligence. He worked hard, tackled back, scurried around the central areas of the field looking for the ball and shouldered his share of the defensive duties. He had a provocative edge to his game that brought him into conflict once or twice with opponents and referees. He tended to niggle the opposition. I always reckoned him to be a very hard, uncompromising player. There was no way, for instance, that he would be intimidated by an aggressive early challenge from a full back. If you caught him with a tackle early on, he always made sure that you realised that it wasn't going to rattle him in the least and that his turn would come.

In his first season he helped City to win the Second Division title and then in a three year spell between 1968 and 1970 – the most successful period in the club's history – he played a significant role in City's triumphs. They won the First Division title, the FA Cup and the European Cup-winners' Cup. Those were the years of the Joe Mercer–Malcolm Allison management partnership. The colourful Allison eventually took sole control and, with a team that included Rodney Marsh, Francis Lee and Colin Bell, the lads from Maine Road finally emerged from the shadow of the mighty Manchester United.

Mike certainly enjoyed the limelight. A confident, almost arrogant player, he had a swagger off the field that was totally in keeping with the times. It was the George Best era at Manchester and Mike was one of the main supporting actors in the social swirl of the time. He had his own shirt business and was a big pal of Bobby Moore, who bought all his shirts from Mike. Manchester was a lively football city in those days and Mike loved the glamour of it all. City's attacking power was their strength at the time and Summerbee's forays on the right, supported by the running of the more orthodox winger Tony Coleman on the left, gave their game a compelling urgency that few other First Division teams could equal. Mike scored his share of goals – 46 in 355 League games for City – and when they had injuries he could also deputise as a central striker. He spent 10 years with City, winning eight England caps, before moving to Burnley in 1975. He then had a brief spell with Blackpool and finished his career as player–manager of Stockport County.

Mike Summerbee was an aggressive and combative figure for Manchester City during the golden years of the Joe Mercer–Malcolm Allison management partnership.

PETER THOMPSON

Peter Thompson (winger)
Carlisle 27.11.42
Preston North End, Liverpool,
Bolton Wanderers
England – 16

Peter Thompson was a wonderful player, one of the most talented wingers of the 1960s and, in my opinion, one of the all-time greats of the Bill Shankly era. Born in Carlisle, Peter began his career with Preston North End in 1959, the year that the legendary Tom Finney retired after spending his entire career at Deepdale. Shankly, spotting the potential in the wiry youth with greyhound-like speed, saw him as a key element in his team rebuilding plans at Liverpool and signed him for £40,000 in August 1963. He was an immediate success, helping Liverpool to win the First Division title in 1963–64. It was the first sign of the coming domination of modern football by the Liverpool club.

Roger Hunt looks on as Peter Thompson shoots, for a change. Peter is remembered most for his darting, elusive runs along the wing for Liverpool and England – until the advent of Alf Ramsey's 1966 'wingless wonders'.

Two seasons later Liverpool won the championship again, Thompson playing in 40 games and giving the team a cutting edge that few could match in Division One. The accuracy of his crosses played a central role in establishing Roger Hunt as one of the most feared strikers of the time. Hunt scored 27 goals in that First Division campaign. This, of course, was the season in which England won the World Cup and, although Hunt was fortunate enough to play a leading role, Thompson had to watch the unfolding drama from the sidelines. He was one of the most conspicuous victims of Alf Ramsey's decision to play without wingers. He had made his international debut against Portugal in 1964 and was a regular in the side throughout most of the next two years.

A fine performance in the 1965 FA Cup final win over Leeds United enhanced his reputation as one of the outstanding wingers of the day, but Ramsey was singularly unimpressed and remained firm in his conviction that the England team was better served by four hard-working midfield players. Thompson played in the 2–1 win over Northern Ireland at Wembley in November 1965 but, in the following match against Spain, Alan Ball wore the number seven shirt. The rest is history. He never again played a significant role in the England side though he continued to make the occasional appearance. His last cap, the sixteenth, was against Scotland in 1970. In the previous seven years he had been one of the country's best orthodox wingers, and one of the last, but that is probably what cost him a place in England's World Cup side.

There was no disputing Peter's quality. He was a fantastic winger; he could take on defenders in tight situations and go past them with ease and he had speed, cunning and superb ball control. I've played against him when he has run the West Ham defence ragged. We knew how he would play and we detailed people to mark him but he could be so sharp and elusive that at times he was simply impossible to contain. Thompson was one of the few wingers to survive after the 1966 World Cup. The tendency to string three of four players across the width of the pitch gradually eroded the value of wingers and those who persevered found that the service they once received was now being stifled by the strength of the opposing midfield.

In those days most wingers faced the choice of either adopting a more functional working role or disappearing altogether. Some, I'm glad to say, survived and Thompson was one of them. Generally, the game became far less entertaining with the emphasis on the midfield play and the few crowd-pleasers in the game were appreciated. The Anfield crowd loved Thompson and rightly so; when I recall the way he had West Ham chasing shadows when we visited Liverpool I can understand why he was so popular and why he remains one of the Liverpool folk heroes. His Liverpool career ended after around 400 games, 50 goals and an appearance as substitute in the 1971 FA Cup final against Arsenal. He later moved down to the Second Division where his playing days finally came to an end with Bolton Wanderers in 1977.

COLIN TODD

Colin Todd (centre back)
Chester-le-Street 12.12.48
Sunderland, Derby County,
Everton, Birmingham City,
Nottingham Forest, Oxford
United
England – 27

I first came across Colin when I went to Turkey with the England youth team in 1967. It was really hot there and I was having trouble with blisters on the balls of my feet. One of the blisters became infected and I couldn't play in the semi-finals of the tournament so Colin was brought into the side. He was an old fashioned type of wing half and he played superbly in that semi-final. Even in those early days he was quick and sharp, a sure tackler and never flamboyant in his use of the ball. He used to win the tackle, play a simple pass and then feel that he had done his job. He was a very effective player so I was not surprised that after his performance in that youth tournament semi-final he kept his place for the final despite the fact that I was fit.

Colin was then at Sunderland and it wasn't until Derby County paid £170,000 for him in 1971 that he won the first of his 27 England senior caps. He made his debut for England at right back against Northern Ireland the following year and moved to the centre of the defence when Bobby Moore retired from the international scene. He was 22 at the time and began partnering his Derby County team-mate Roy McFarland in the middle of the England defence. It was a formidable pairing at club level and it would have been equally effective at international level had it not been for the injuries that McFarland suffered.

Colin was a super player in his own right and should have been an England centre back for at least 10 years. It has always been a little bit of a mystery to me why he didn't become a greater player. In the early 1970s when he was in the England team and Derby had a championship winning team he looked as though he could have reached Bobby Moore's status. But he probably suffered in the early part of his international career because of the consistent excellence of Moore, who played 108 times for England, and Norman Hunter of Leeds United. He had to be patient, but I think the waiting may have taken a little of the edge off his appetite. And then, just as he was settled in the side, along came Phil Thompson, flushed with Liverpool's success, to challenge Colin for his place. He had many outstanding qualities but he was unfortunate to be around at the same time as several other fine defenders. He was one of the hardest defenders to get away from. If you got past him you could guarantee that within a few yards he would be back snapping at your heels. He had electric pace for a defender and was one of those players who would never concede that you had him beaten.

If I had a criticism of him it was that he was largely a defensive player with little attacking instinct. Having won the ball and passed it to a team-mate he seemed to say, 'Right, that's me done. Now get on with it.' Perhaps that's why he didn't win more caps although his reputation at club level remained unimpaired. After nine seasons at Derby he had two indifferent years with Everton and then played for Birmingham, Nottingham Forest and Oxford. Soon after hanging up his boots he joined his former Derby team-mate Bruce Rioch at Middlesbrough. Bruce was manager at Ayresome Park and appointed Colin as his assistant. Together they lifted the club from the jaws of the liquidators to the Third Division title in 1987 and followed that by clinching a First Division place a year later with play-off victories over Bradford City and Chelsea.

*The sharp-tackling Colin Todd.
His partnership with Roy
McFarland in the heart of Derby's
defence was one of the most
formidable I ever faced.*

JOHN TOSHACK

John Toshack MBE (striker)
Cardiff 22.3.49
Cardiff City, Liverpool,
Swansea City
Wales – 40

John Toshack was a towering figure in the Liverpool team which enjoyed phenomenal success in the 1970s. He was 6 ft 1 in tall, competitive and athletic and the partnership he established with Kevin Keegan made the pair of them the most feared attacking force in the First Division. Kevin spent six years playing alongside John at Anfield, and loved every moment of it. He has always given 'Tosh' a lot of the credit for his own success at Liverpool. As a partnership they were almost impossible to contain successfully, as we discovered at West Ham; we were never able to control them. Some of the more imaginative newspapers at the time claimed that they had some strange telepathic understanding and, to be honest, it wouldn't have surprised me. Tosh won the high balls and Kevin, so quick and busy, was almost invariably first to reach his knock-downs.

John was born in Cardiff and showed an early aptitude for cricket, which isn't really surprising because a distant relative, Ernie Toshack, was an Australian Test cricketer who played against England nine times in the years immediately after the Second World War. John played for the Welsh Schoolboy XI but football was his first love and he went to his home town club as an apprentice, breaking into the first team in 1965–66 when he scored six goals in his first eight games. The following season he scored 10 goals in 22 games and, thus, set the pattern of a goal every other game that was to continue for his six years at Cardiff. He made quite a stir as a marksman in the Second Division and in March 1968 Bobby Robson, then manager of Fulham, just failed in a bid to sign him. 'Now watch the big clubs move in for him', said Robson at the time. But it was another two years before Liverpool persuaded Cardiff to part with him and it cost them a club record fee of £110,000. Bill Shankly, who signed him for Liverpool, always considered Tosh to be one of his shrewdest buys.

In seven seasons at Anfield he scored 94 goals in nearly 250 appearances. He played in three League championship triumphs and received winners' medals in the FA Cup, the European Cup, though he didn't play in the final against Borussia Moenchengladbach in 1977, and the UEFA Cup twice. It was his heading ability that won him most acclaim. Apart from setting up chances for Keegan, he established a reputation for scoring with far post headers. For a big man he also had a deceptively neat touch on the ground which wasn't always appreciated.

He had made his international debut for Wales while at Cardiff but the bulk of his 40 caps, and 13 goals, came during his years at Anfield. The last of his international appearances came in 1979, by which time he was at Swansea playing in the lower reaches of the Football League. He had suffered with his share of injuries at Liverpool – a £140,000 move to Leicester was called off at the last minute in 1974 because he failed a medical examination – and by 1978 a knee problem meant that he was spending more time in the Anfield treatment room than on the pitch. Liverpool had

OPPOSITE *John Toshack's aerial ability continually caused problems for defences, and his partnership with Kevin Keegan was feared throughout the country.*

asked £80,000 when Norwich, Newcastle and the Belgian club Anderlecht tried to sign him. But when Swansea, chipping out an existence in Division Four, asked him to be their player–manager, Liverpool decided to release him on a free transfer in recognition of his services, and so began a completely new chapter in Toshack's remarkable career. That was in March 1978 and his first game for Swansea in Division Four was against Watford. He scored in a 3–3 draw. In all he scored six goals in 13 games at the end of that season, helping Swansea to clinch third place and promotion to the Third Division.

The rest of the story is recorded for posterity in the record books. In a three year spell with Toshack at the helm Swansea climbed from the Fourth Division to the First – a feat unrivalled in League history. To help him he called upon the experience of former Liverpool colleagues like Tommy Smith, Ian Callaghan, Ray Kennedy, Phil Boersma and Alan Waddle and at one time, when Swansea actually sat at the top of the First Division and were competing in Europe, Toshack was being tipped as the next manager at Anfield. But sadly it all went wrong for him. The team he had built disintegrated at an alarming rate and his spending in the transfer market meant that the club had debts of more than £1 million when they were relegated from Division One in 1983. In November of that year Swansea were bottom of Division Two with just one win from their opening 16 games. Toshack resigned with 18 months of his contract to run and he asked for no compensation.

Eight weeks later he accepted an invitation to return on half his original salary but this time there were no miracles. He lasted eight weeks and was sacked; Swansea were relegated to Division Three and their decline continued but Tosh bounced back. In 1986 he accepted a job as manager of Spanish club Real Sociedad. In his first season they beat favourites Atletico Madrid in the Spanish Cup final.

DAVE WATSON

Dave was a tremendous centre half, a granite-like pillar in the heart of the England defence, but one of the things I will always remember him for was his love of heavy rock music. When the England team was travelling you always knew which hotel room Dave was in because he took with him a radio cassette player with big speakers and you could usually hear the music all the way down the corridor. His favourite group at the time was Status Quo and with his long hair and craggy, distinctive features I could imagine him twanging a guitar on stage. He often went to recording studios to listen to bands making records and was almost as serious about music as he was about football.

He had started his soccer career as a striker with Notts County but it was under Tommy Docherty at Rotherham that he began to blossom into a quality centre half. He was a nice guy and a super centre half – very consistent and very strong. When Roy McFarland dropped out of the England scene with an Achilles' tendon injury, Dave was the natural

Dave Watson (centre back)
Stapleford 5.10.46
Notts County, Rotherham
United, Sunderland,
Manchester City, Werder
Bremen, Southampton, Stoke
City, Derby County
England – 65

Stoke City's Dave Watson and West Ham's Nicky Morgan in a balletic tussle for possession. A cornerstone of the England sides of the 1970s, Dave was one of the best headers of the ball I have seen.

replacement. He made his international debut in 1974 by which time he had established himself in the Sunderland team where he is mainly remembered for the glorious FA Cup final victory the Second Division side secured over hot favourites Leeds United.

Dave was not particulary tall for a centre half but he compensated for that with an excellent spring and good timing which made him a very effective and powerful header of the ball. Few opponents could brush him aside. He always seemed to have the strength and power to keep his balance and retain possession of the ball. He became an essential part of Ron Greenwood's England side and his was one of the first names to go on the team sheet. I thought he was one of England's key players during that era. If he had a fault it was that he was a bit one footed, not only with his passing but with his tackling, too, but he did get his right leg in where it hurt and when he tackled you, you knew all about it. He didn't just look intimidating, he was intimidating. He was a tough guy who marked some of the world's best strikers during a 65-match international career. I remember the two of us making our debut together in Sir Alf Ramsey's last match as manager, against Portugal in Lisbon in 1974.

Don Revie, Ramsey's successor, played him regularly and Greenwood thought the world of him. He kept him in the squad until the 1982 World Cup, by which time he was 35. Dave had joined Manchester City from Sunderland, played briefly for Werder Bremen in West Germany, then spent three seasons at Southampton before moving on to Stoke and Derby. Dave, a big hearted player struggling with a knee problem, was still pulling on his boots at 38.

JOHN WHITE

John White was one of the reasons that I used to take the bus to White Hart Lane on some Saturday afternoons in the early 1960s. He became one of the key players in the wonderful Spurs side that achieved the League and FA Cup double in 1961, but died three years later at the age of 27, a career of immense promise still unfulfilled.

John White (midfield)
Musselburgh 28.4.37
died 21.7.64
Falkirk, Tottenham Hotspur
Scotland — 22

John was born in Musselburgh and played for Falkirk before becoming one of Bill Nicholson's first signings for Tottenham in 1959 at a fee of £20,000. He was a slightly built, shy, enigmatic Scot. They called him 'the Ghost' at Spurs because of the way he used to glide almost unnoticed into positions. It was his touch, vision and passing that I and thousands of others came to admire. His qualities complemented perfectly the contribution made by his rugged fellow Scot, Dave Mackay. Once Mackay had broken up an opposing attack, White and Danny Blanchflower took over, providing the creative impetus that made that Spurs side one of the most entertaining in the game's history. John was an old fashioned inside forward who used to wear number eight. Primarily right footed, he could chip a ball onto a sixpence and his passes created many of the openings that helped to produce an incredible total of 115 goals in the First Division in the double season. He played in all 42 League matches that season and scored 13 goals himself.

John was a similar player to Ray Wilkins from a passing point of view. They had the same ability to strike a long or short pass with slide-rule accuracy, or chip the ball with equal effect. I used to marvel at the way his long passes opened up the opposing defences. He had a great influence on the early years of my career and I would have loved the opportunity to play against him. Sadly that never happened and I can still remember reading about his death in the newspapers. He was found dead under an oak tree at Crews Hill Golf Club where he had been struck by lightning. Like many Scottish footballers he was a competent golfer, playing off a handicap of 14, and he had gone alone to the course to practise. When the storm struck he sheltered under a tree with a towel draped around his shoulders. The verdict at the inquest was misadventure. The coroner said that if someone with medical training had been nearby John's heart might have been revived.

His death was a great loss to Spurs in particular, and to the game in general. He was one of the great players of his day and who knows what he might have achieved had he lived. He had played 22 times for Scotland and scored 46 goals in 200 games over five years with Spurs. Those who played with or against him reckon that he still had to reach the peak of his potential. Nicholson, who helped to arrange a memorial match against a Scottish XI for John's family, believes that he would have played into his 30s. In Nicholson's book about his life with Tottenham he said of John, 'He was fit because he was a cross-country runner and he was very energetic. He could control the ball from any angle and in such a way that a defender couldn't take it off him. Ron Flowers used to complain that he could never get near him. As the ball arrived, White would turn away from him, denying him a chance to get in a tackle'.

Although White was a retiring sort of chap, Nicholson recalls that he was something of a practical joker and rarely missed an opportunity to show off his skill in the dressing room. He used to flip a half-crown piece up from his foot to his forehead, let it drop back to his foot and then flip it up again and catch it in his pocket. Inevitably his death hastened the break-up of the great double side. It had been at its peak for less than four years but few teams stay together for much longer than that. Had John lived, he would have been young enough and good enough to have provided the foundation stone for Nicholson's rebuilding of the team.

One of Bill Nicholson's first signings for Tottenham, John White had won 22 Scottish caps and had scored 46 goals in 200 games for Spurs before his tragic death at the age of 27. Observers maintain that he still had not reached his peak.

RAY WILKINS

Any player who makes 82 appearances for England in a 10 year international career has to be pretty special, and for me Ray Wilkins is special. I've never really understood the criticism that he's received from fans and the media in the last couple of seasons for his style of play. I think people have been a little unfair to him, saying that he plays too many square and backward passes. It became fashionable to claim that he played too deep and Ron

Ray Wilkins (midfield)
Hillingdon 14.9.56
Chelsea, Manchester United,
AC Milan, Paris St Germain,
Glasgow Rangers
England – 84

Mexico, 1986: frustration and despair for Ray Wilkins as he is sent off following an uncharacteristic incident in England's World Cup match against Morocco. It was a sad end to the international career of a quality player, famous for his passing ability.

Atkinson, the manager who sold Ray from Manchester United to AC Milan, did him no favours by describing him as a crab because he reckoned that Ray always passed sideways. What people have tended to forget is the quality of his football and the number of outstanding games that he has played for his country. From the very outset it was clear that he was going to be no ordinary player.

Ray came from a footballing family; his father, George, played professionally before the war and his three sons, Ray, Graham and Dean, all followed in his footsteps, but Ray was the most talented. He was an England schoolboy star before turning professional with Chelsea in 1973. Like many people, I was surprised when the Chelsea manager, Dave Sexton, made him club captain at the age of 18 but, meeting Ray later, I understood Dave's reasoning. Ray was a popular, charming and diplomatic lad who seemed to thrive on the responsibility of captaincy; other players liked him, and they responded to him. His passing ability, for me, was his greatest attribute. He could hit a great long ball, the sort of pass that would open up an opposing defence and create a goalscoring chance. He was a perfectionist, a player who hated to lose possession of the ball. He was also a very patient player who would hit an easy pass sideways to retain possession rather than risk losing the ball because of an unpredictable long pass.

He rarely gave the ball away and that is a great quality in any player. He played the game in the Liverpool fashion and I could never understand why he was criticised for that. Of course, when he had good runners up front, moving into space, he could hit them with long penetrative passes. He could tackle soundly, but not outstandingly for a midfield player. He was probably England's best player in the European Championship in Italy in 1980. One of the best games of his career was against Belgium when he scored a super goal. Sadly, it's a match most people remember for the terrace rioting and the tear gas. He was a key figure in two World Cups and it's a great shame that his international career ended in the way it did in Mexico in 1986. He was sent off during the goalless draw against Morocco. The fact that Bryan Robson was injured in the same match only made matters worse for England. I was at the game and can't make any excuses for a player of Ray's experience. He threw the ball at the referee — an uncharacteristic incident, but one that was seen by a worldwide television audience. That's what they will remember him for when in fact he deserves to be remembered for the quality of his football.

He played in the first international of the following season — a disappointing 1–0 defeat in Sweden, and was then left out. That seemed to be the end of an illustrious international career. But there's no doubt in my mind that, in a side of the correct blend, Ray was a wonderful player with a big match temperament and the ability to hit passes that few other players in the world could surpass. Others obviously thought so, too. At the start of the 1987–88 season Paris St Germain thought enough of him to sign him from AC Milan, but after a few months he joined the other English exiles serving under Graeme Souness at Glasgow Rangers.

RAY WILSON

Ray Wilson secured his place in the game's folklore when he played in the England side that beat West Germany in the 1966 World Cup final at Wembley. He formed an outstanding full back partnership for England at that time with Fulham's George Cohen. They played together on the international stage on 28 occasions and many observers rate them as the best England full back combination of all time. Ray won a total of 63 caps which was a record for an England full back for nearly 20 years until it was surpassed by Arsenal's Kenny Sansom.

Ray was a compact figure, small neat and tough. He came from Derbyshire but learned the basics of his trade at Huddersfield Town, a club that had a reputation for producing good full backs. It was his good fortune to come under the expert eye of coach Roy Goodall, who with Sam Wadsworth had formed a legendary full back partnership in the Town side that won the League title in three successive seasons between 1924–26.

Ray was a forward of limited potential when he returned from National Service in 1955 and it was Goodall who switched him so successfully to full back. It turned out to be the making of his career. He soon became a regular fixture at left back in Huddersfield's Second Division team and within a couple of seasons it was obvious that he was going to become the best left back in the country. He stayed with Huddersfield for nine seasons during which time he was courted by all the big First Division clubs but, even though he made regular demands for a move, the Yorkshire club was adamant that he should stay with them. Finally, in 1964, they relented and sold him to Everton for £40,000.

He had made his England debut four years earlier and by this time was a regular in Alf Ramsey's team. He was a composed, diligent defender who always looked in command, even in the most frenzied situations. His marking was tight, his tackling crisp and his distribution accurate without being over-elaborate. He knew what he was good at and tried to play to his strengths. If he had a weakness it was his heading. It was his tame headed clearance that gave West Germany's Helmut Haller the chance to open the scoring in the 1966 final at Wembley. But, such was Ray's character and ability, that he hardly put a foot wrong from that moment on. Earlier in the tournament his intelligent pass had begun the move that led to Geoff Hurst's winning goal in the quarter-finals against Argentina and he played a major role in the first of England's goals in their semi-final win over Portugal. He was 32 when he played in the World Cup final and, while that was unquestionably the peak of his career, he enjoyed memorable moments during his five seasons with Everton, most notably two FA Cup final appearances against Sheffield Wednesday in 1966 and WBA in 1968.

He was one of the most reliable full backs I can remember watching and he seemed to have the happy knack of initiating vital attacking moves as he did for Hurst on that famous occasion against Argentina in 1966. Cohen

Ray Wilson (full back)
Shirebrook 17.12.34
Huddersfield Town, Everton, Oldham Athletic, Bradford City
England — 63

was a more dashing figure, catching the eye with his charges along the right flank, but Wilson was the more complete full back — a master-tradesman who did his job with unerring certainty. In 1969 at the age of 35 he joined Oldham for a season and a year later went to Bradford City as player–coach for a short time. In a 15-year career he played just over 400 games and would probably had played many more had he not been so unlucky with injuries. When he finally retired from the game in 1970 he built up a successful career as an undertaker.

England's Ray Wilson in control in a friendly against Brazil in 1963. He always impressed with his crisp tackling and all-round composure.

FRANK WORTHINGTON

Tall, unorthodox and fiercely independent, Frank was one of the game's most gifted and colourful strikers during my years as a professional. He was a player I enjoyed watching and one I would like to have played alongside on a regular basis. I played with him on a couple of occasions in the England team and it was my belief that he should have been a regular member of the side; as it was he won only eight caps. His off the field image is something that probably didn't help his chances of international selection. He was a lively character, inclined to dress outrageously and ignore many of the niceties that professional footballers have to observe from time to time. It was his individualism that made him so good to watch on the football field. His brushes with the game's authorities did nothing to dilute his belief that football was a sport to be enjoyed and he intended to enjoy it. His desire to entertain burned as strongly as his desire to win and wherever he played he became a great favourite with the crowds.

Frank Worthington (striker)
Halifax 23.11.48
Huddersfield Town, Leicester City, Bolton Wanderers, Birmingham City, Leeds United, Sunderland, Southampton, Brighton and Hove Albion, Tranmere Rovers, Preston North End, Stockport County
England – 8

He had a wonderful left foot, a great touch and ball control that you would more often see in South American players. He liked to roll the ball under his foot, dragging it away from defenders before releasing a terrific shot. My first memories of him date back to his Huddersfield days when he played in the same side as Trevor Cherry. It was obvious even then that both would move on to bigger things. There was a chance that he could have joined West Ham when he left Huddersfield after six years in 1972. Ron Greenwood, then the manager at Upton Park, was keen to sign him, but Liverpool and Leicester were interested, too. When he failed a medical at Anfield West Ham's interest faded, but Leicester persevered and signed him for £80,000. He spent five years at Filbert Street where he became a key member of Jimmy Bloomfield's fine team along with other entertainers like Alan Birchenall, Keith Weller and Jon Sammels.

At Huddersfield he had won a Second Division championship medal in 1970, but the major honours eluded him at Leicester City. Their playing style made them exciting and good to watch but they lacked the killer instinct of some of the more successful teams of the time. Frank spent six seasons at Leicester before moving to Bolton and Birmingham where he helped both clubs to achieve First Division status. In 1982 he resumed his travels, moving to Leeds for two seasons, before joining Sunderland and then Southampton. He later played in the United States but returned to become player–manager of Tranmere and, after getting the sack there, he played for Preston at the age of 38. As he approached his fortieth birthday he was still playing for Stockport County in Division Four.

Some would have accused him of being unprofessional and had his attitude been a little less frivolous I'm sure he would have become a regular in the England side. Sadly, his rebellious nature worked against him, though it never stopped him from scoring. Throughout his career his goalscoring rate was consistent at around one every three games. He was a happy-go-

Frank Worthington's desire to entertain burned as strongly as his desire to win.

lucky character, one of three footballing brothers from Halifax, and a player for whom the game was not the be-all and end-all; his enthusiasm for Elvis Presley was nearly as strong as his love of football. He made no secret of the fact that Presley was his idol and he knew everything there was to know about the rock and roller.

BILLY WRIGHT

Every school playground in the 1950s had a little bunch of lads who supported Wolves. They were one of the glamour sides of that era and by far the most glamorous name in a very fine team was that of Billy Wright, captain of England. Wright was one of the all-time great England captains and the first man to play more than 100 games for his country. When he retired in 1959 he had played 105 internationals, a record that was beaten by Bobby Charlton 11 years later.

His fair, wavy hair and robust tackling made him one of the great stars of the post-war soccer scene. There was a time though when Wolves, his only club, doubted that he would make the grade in the professional game. They had signed him straight from school and came close to sending him home because he was not considered big enough for the rigours of the game. It was ironic, then, that he should become one of England's most successful centre halves. He was only 5 ft 8 in but was converted from wing half to the centre back position largely because of his ability to spring into the air to meet high balls.

Neil Franklin was unchallenged as the England number five immediately after the war but when he went to play in Bogota the selectors had to find a replacement. They eventually settled on Billy, who had been playing alongside Franklin in the England half back line. Ron Greenwood, my old manager with West Ham and England, and a man who often played against Wright, believes that his move to centre half when Franklin went abroad extended his international career quite significantly. Billy was a busy, uncomplicated type of player and, although not a great passer, it's Ron's opinion that he was one of the best ball winners of his era. 'He had a great attitude and his powers of motivation made him an outstanding captain', said Greenwood. 'Playing in the middle of the defence, of course, also meant that he didn't have to cover quite so much ground as he did at wing half.'

Billy made his England debut in 1946 and such was his consistency at the peak of his career that between 1951 and 1959 he played 70 consecutive international matches — a record that is most unlikely to fall. Domestically, his career was just as successful; Wolves were among the pioneers of European football in the 1950s and, as a youngster, I can recall being enthralled by clips of their televised games against Moscow Dynamo. As a wing half he was a player who did the simple things strikingly well, but it was as a centre half that he earned his place in the game's history books. He was 30 when he first made the switch for England in the 1954 World Cup finals in Switzerland, but he was an instant success. The defensive burden was heavier, but he relished the responsibility. His reading of the game, his weighty tackling and his punchy heading made him a leader others wanted to follow. He was captain of the Wolves side that beat Leicester in the 1949 FA Cup final and two years later he was voted

Billy Wright CBE (centre back)
Ironbridge 6.2.24
Wolverhampton Wanderers
England — 105

Footballer of the Year. Then he led Wolves to three League title triumphs in 1954, 1958 and 1959.

His reputation throughout his career was spotless and he was a fine example to all youngsters. He was one of Britain's great sporting heroes in the post-war years and, much to the delight of the nation, married Joy Beverley of the singing Beverley Sisters. Billy later became a successful television executive. The Billy Wright story is the stuff of fiction; the foundry worker's son who was first told he was too small and then recovered from a badly broken ankle to become a genuine sporting goliath. He chose to retire in a characteristically quiet manner, after a club trial game at the start of season 1959–60. When he was no longer the best, he knew it was time to go.

Billy Wright, idol of the assembled youngsters, emerges from the tunnel for the 1959 England v Scotland match in which he became the first England player to reach 100 caps.

ALEX YOUNG

Alex Young is a striker I have always remembered for his composure, elegance and touch on the ball. He was arguably the greatest Scottish player ever to sign for Everton. He came from Loanhead and left Hearts to join Everton for £40,000 in 1960. He spent seven years at Goodison Park and scored 77 goals in 228 First Division matches. His blond hair made him a distinctive figure on the field and the fans called him the 'Golden Vision' which was a wonderfully appropriate name.

In tight attacking situations he always seemed to have that little bit more time than other players. He knew which way to turn and where to play the

Alex Young (striker)
Loanhead 3.2.37
Heart of Midlothian, Everton,
Glentoran, Stockport County
Scotland — 8

Alex Young, a gifted, elegant striker, was idolised by the Everton fans — when he was replaced near the end of his career there was a public outcry!

ball almost instinctively. He was one of the players who impressed upon me the value of vision, of being aware of what was going on around you.

Sometimes, when I was watching him hit a pass, I'd think that he was pretty lucky because the ball arrived at the feet of a team-mate even though Alex hadn't looked up before hitting it. When he did the same thing a second time, and then a third time, I realised that he didn't have to look where he was passing; he was aware of all the options without looking up. As a young player in the 1960s I was in awe of this ability that set Alex apart from so many other players. Soon afterwards my manager at West Ham, Ron Greenwood, would frequently underline the value of having that kind of vision. One of his great coaching theories was simply that players should always have a picture in their mind of what was going on around them before receiving the ball. His point was that a player who was aware of the options at the time of receiving the ball did not have to look up for a team-mate before passing.

A lot of my enthusiasm as a youngster was generated by going along on a Saturday afternoon to study players like Alex Young. Sadly, as the hooligan problem developed, many parents prevented their children from going to watch games. I often wonder whether there are any kids left who race home from a match and go out into the back garden to try to emulate the players they have just seen. That's what I used to do because, although I was a budding young midfield player, Alex had many qualities that I admired. A lot of strikers in those days were the old-time battlers, but Alex had a little bit of subtlety and style and far more natural ability than many gave him credit for. He was a major influence in the Everton side that won the First Division title in 1963 and the side that beat Sheffield Wednesday 3–2 in the FA Cup final at Wembley three years later. For all his talent, though, he played only eight times for Scotland, which was always a bit of a mystery to me.

Such was his popularity at Goodison Park that when the manager of the time, Harry Catterick, sensed that Alex was coming to the end of his career and replaced him with a youngster called Joe Royle, he was assaulted by outraged Everton supporters. But in 1967 Everton released him and he played briefly for Glentoran in Northern Ireland before returning to the Football League for a final season with Stockport County in 1968–69.

Alex remains a popular figure in Scottish football and I was delighted to learn recently that his son, Jason, had joined his father's old club, Hearts, on schoolboy forms. Perhaps up in Edinburgh they hope that Jason can help restore the days of glory the club enjoyed when Alex was playing. They won the Scottish championship twice in three seasons – in 1958 and 1960, when Alex was an influential figure in the team. Since then there have been few significant additions to the trophy cabinet at Tynecastle Park, although in the late 1980s they showed encouraging signs of breaking the Rangers–Celtic domination.